JESUS and MATTHEW

JESUS and MATTHEW

Faithful Jews

Margaret Nutting Ralph

Paulist Press
New York / Mahwah, NJ

Cover image: Caravaggio, *The Calling of St. Matthew,* 1599–1600; photographed by VivaItalia1974 / Wikimedia Commons
Cover design by Sharyn Banks
Book design by Lynn Else

Library of Congress Cataloging-in-Publication Data
Names: Ralph, Margaret Nutting, author.
Title: Jesus and Matthew: faithful Jews / Margaret Nutting Ralph.
Description: New York/Mahwah, NJ: Paulist Press, [2024] | Includes index. | Summary: "This book explains the Old Testament allusions used in the Gospel of Matthew in their original contexts, thus casting light on the messages Matthew seeks to teach about Jesus"—Provided by publisher.
Identifiers: LCCN 2023057115 (print) | LCCN 2023057116 (ebook) | ISBN 9780809157013 (paperback) | ISBN 9780809188703 (ebook)
Subjects: LCSH: Bible. Matthew—Criticism, interpretation, etc. | Jesus Christ—Person and offices—Biblical teaching. | Bible. Old Testament—Quotations in the New Testament. | Bible. Matthew—Relation to the Old Testament.
Classification: LCC BS2575.52 .R35 2024 (print) | LCC BS2575.52 (ebook) | DDC 226.2/06—dc23/eng/20240611
LC record available at https://lccn.loc.gov/2023057115
LC ebook record available at https://lccn.loc.gov/2023057116]

ISBN 978-0-8091-5701-3 (paperback)
ISBN 978-0-8091-8870-3 (e-book)

Published by Paulist Press
997 Macarthur Boulevard
Mahwah, New Jersey 07430
www.paulistpress.com

Printed and bound in the
United States of America

CONTENTS

PREFACE

The idea for this book came to me after hearing two comments from friends. The first was, "I see no need to read the Old Testament. The New Testament has replaced it. So, all I need to know I can learn from reading the New Testament." The second was, "It is so hard to believe that Jesus felt abandoned by his Father on the cross. However, he obviously did, or he wouldn't have cried out, 'My God, my God, why have you forsaken me?'"

I believe that we cannot understand the good news that we read in the Gospels if we have no knowledge of the Old Testament. Why? Because Gospel authors are constantly alluding to Old Testament texts. If we don't understand the allusions, we have no way of understanding the Gospel author's intent.

What is an allusion? Well, say that I am reading a novel in which one character thinks that another character is a little full of himself. So, the first character says, "He thinks there was a star over his birthplace." For a Christian who is familiar with the Gospel according to Matthew, that comment is perfectly clear. Those who recognize the reference, the allusion to Matthew's Gospel, would understand the intent behind the comment. Those who do not recognize the allusion might well misunderstand the intent. Was the comment intended to mean that the person thought he was destined to be an astronomer?

If we read the New Testament without any knowledge of the Old Testament, we will miss the meaning of the authors' many allusions to the Old Testament, and therefore we will miss what the authors are intending to teach. This is important because, when interpreting Scripture, we put the authority of Scripture behind the intent of the inspired authors.

A perfect illustration of the importance of understanding Old Testament allusions in order to understand what an author is teaching is Matthew's passion narrative (Mark's, too), in which Jesus cries from the cross, "My God, my God, why have you forsaken me?" (Matt 27:46). Has Jesus lost faith in his Father's love and presence? No. Matthew is picturing Jesus beginning to pray Psalm 22, a psalm of lament. Laments start with a call to God and a complaint, but they move on to an expression of trust, a petition, and praise for God's mighty saving power.

Psalm 22 concludes with a long and magnificent song of praise:

> All the ends of the earth shall remember
>   and turn to the LORD;
> and all the families of the nations
>   shall worship before him.
> For dominion belongs to the LORD,
>   and he rules over the nations.
> To him, indeed, shall all who sleep in the earth bow down;
>   before him shall bow all who go down to the dust,
>   and I shall live for him.
> Posterity will serve him;
>   future generations will be told about the Lord,
> and proclaim his deliverance to people yet unborn,
>   saying that he has done it.

By picturing Jesus praying Psalm 22, Matthew is not only describing Jesus's suffering, but he is also teaching his readers the significance of Jesus's crucifixion and death. Jesus redeemed the whole world. All the families of nations have come to know their God through Jesus Christ. Future generations, including ours, have heard of their deliverance. How much more meaningful are Jesus's words when we understand the allusion to the Old Testament!

In this book we will examine Old Testament allusions in the Gospel according to Matthew. Why choose Matthew? It is true that many New Testament books could be used to illustrate this same point. However, in Matthew, Old Testament allusions are constantly present because Matthew is addressing a primarily Jewish audience for whom the meaning of these allusions would be self-evident.

Matthew's Gospel starts with a genealogy that places his whole Gospel in the context of Old Testament salvation history. Matthew's theme is that Jesus is the new Moses who has authority from God to teach a new law. Some biblical scholars suggest that the structure of Matthew's Gospel, following the genealogy and the birth narratives and preceding the passion narrative, consists of five sections, each including a narrative about Jesus and a discourse by Jesus, the five sections reflecting the five books of the Pentateuch in the Old Testament. Of all New Testament books, Matthew's Gospel most depends on knowledge of the Old Testament in order to be fully understood. A study of Matthew's Gospel will clearly illustrate that the New Testament has not replaced the Old Testament. Rather, the New Testament relies on the Old Testament and tells us the rest of the story.

One final introductory comment: You may have noticed that I previously said that Matthew and Mark picture Jesus praying Psalm 22. This wording might cause you to ask, "Are you suggesting that Jesus did not actually say these words while on the cross?" This question brings up the topic of literary form, or genre. What kind of writing is Matthew's Gospel? We will respond to this question in our first chapter.

The question also gives me an opportunity to explain my field of study. My PhD is not in theology nor in biblical studies. Rather, my doctorate is in English literature, a degree I pursued in order to apply knowledge of literary forms (What genre is Matthew's Gospel?) and literary devices (Matthew's use of allusions) to biblical texts. I have found that knowledge of literary forms and literary devices is extremely illuminating when reading biblical texts. I hope you will, too.

ACKNOWLEDGMENTS

As I wrote this book, in which I explore the significance of the Old Testament allusions in the Gospel according to Matthew, I became more and more aware of the deep debt of gratitude we all have to those in previous generations who have devoted themselves to biblical scholarship.

I respond to many questions in this book that interested readers ask: Who are the Pharisees, the Scribes, the Sadducees? What does a particular Hebrew or Greek word mean? How was Passover celebrated in Jesus's time? All of this factual information is available to all of us because of the scholarly work of previous generations. I would like to name two biblical commentaries and two biblical dictionaries that I have relied on over the years:

- The *New Jerome Biblical Commentary* published by Prentice-Hall
- The *Collegeville Bible Commentary* published by Liturgical Press
- The *Mercer Dictionary of the Bible* published by Mercer University Press
- The *Encyclopedic Dictionary of the Bible* published by McGraw-Hill Book Company

In addition, I want to thank my husband, Don, and my son, Tony: Don for constantly encouraging me to keep studying and writing, and Tony for patiently teaching me what I needed to learn about technology.

Finally, I would like to thank my colleagues at Paulist Press, especially my editors, Donna Crilly and Mary Dern Walker.

"I thank my God every time I remember you, constantly praying with joy in every one of my prayers for all of you, because of your sharing in the gospel from the first day until now" (Phil 1:2–5).

1

THE GOSPEL ACCORDING TO…

The first book of the New Testament is titled "The Gospel according to Matthew." This title leads many to assume that the book contains a historical eyewitness account of the life of Jesus. However, the author of this book is not primarily teaching history but theology, and the author is not claiming to be an eyewitness. So, before we explore why knowledge of the Old Testament is essential to our understanding of what the Gospel according to Matthew is teaching, let us first lay a firm foundation for what is to follow in future chapters by responding to several questions:

- What is a Gospel?
- Who wrote the Gospels?
- Why is Matthew's Gospel first in the New Testament?

WHAT IS A GOSPEL?

We have all heard the phrase "the Gospels and the Epistles." We know what an Epistle is; an Epistle is a letter. But what is a Gospel? The word *gospel* means "good news." The word tells us nothing about the kind of writing, that is, the literary form or genre, that we are reading. It is important to know the kind of writing we are reading because, if we misunderstand the literary form, we will misunderstand the intent of the author. If we misunderstand the intent of the author, we will misunderstand the revelation that Christians believe the book contains.

Our New Testament canon includes four works that are called Gospels, and are attributed, respectively, to Matthew, Mark, Luke, and John. The first three have a great deal in common and, for that reason, are referred to as the "Synoptic Gospels." What we say about one in terms of literary form could be said about all three. John differs greatly from the other three. For instance, John's Gospel begins before creation, and it does not picture Jesus teaching in parables but in long theological discourses. The Synoptic Gospels and the Gospel according to John are not the same kind of writing.

Both Matthew's and Luke's Gospels are the result of a five-step process. Matthew does not tell us about this process, but Luke does when he begins his Gospel by saying, "Since many have undertaken to set down an orderly account of the events that have been fulfilled among us, just as they were handed on to us by those who from the beginning were eyewitnesses and servants of the word, I too decided, after investigating everything carefully from the very first, to write an orderly account for you, most excellent Theophilus, so that you may know the truth concerning the things about which you have been instructed" (Luke 1:1–4).

Notice, Luke does not claim to be an eyewitness to the events he describes. Rather, he has relied on the testimony of "those who from the beginning were eyewitnesses and servants of the word." In other words, people before Luke witnessed Jesus's public ministry and passed on accounts through oral tradition. Also, people before Luke undertook "to set down an orderly account of the events" that had been witnessed and passed on through oral tradition. So, a written tradition also existed before Luke. Luke, too, is writing "an orderly account." In other words, Luke is editing inherited oral and written traditions about events, to teach not history but theology, to pass on "the truth concerning the things" about which Theophilus has "been instructed."

Since both Matthew's and Luke's Gospels are edited accounts of earlier oral and written traditions about events that were witnessed, we must ask two questions: How reliable is oral tradition? What written sources did Matthew and Luke use?

IS ORAL TRADITION RELIABLE?

Oral tradition is very reliable. Why? Because it is the product of a community witness, not the product of an individual witness. Oral tradition does not compare to a game that many children play called "telephone" or "gossip," in which one person whispers something to another, that person whispers it to someone else, etcetera. The last person who receives the message says it out loud, and the result is invariably different from the original message. If this game involved speaking out loud rather than whispering, mistakes would be corrected as soon as they were made. For example, if a child prayed out loud, "Our Father, who art in heaven, Harold be thy name," someone would immediately correct the child's mistake.

At the same time, oral tradition does not claim accuracy in exact quotations, in exact social settings, or in exact historical chronological order. Scripture scholars believe that we get closest to hearing Jesus's actual words when we read the parables. Jesus's long theological discourses are not thought to be exact quotations. Rather, they are speeches composed by the author and placed on Jesus's lips to convey what the author had come to know about what Jesus taught during his public ministry. This characteristic of literature that is the fruit of oral tradition explains why, when Jesus is pictured as teaching the Beatitudes in Matthew 5:1–11 and in Luke 6:20–22, the words are not identical. Exact quotes were not an expectation in Jesus's time. In fact, Greek Koine, the language in which the Gospels were originally written, did not have quotation marks. Despite the fact that oral tradition does not claim exact quotations, I will continue to say, "Jesus said," when discussing words attributed to Jesus in the Gospel. I am simply referring to the text, not entering the scholarly debate about which of the words attributed to Jesus are his own words.

Where was Jesus when he taught the Beatitudes? Matthew pictures Jesus on a mountain, and Luke pictures him on a plain. Oral tradition does not claim accuracy in the exact social setting. The author/editor is free to provide the social setting. Scripture scholars think Matthew places Jesus on a mountain as he proclaims a new law to remind his readers that Moses was on a mountain when he promulgated the Law. Matthew, then, wants his readers to think of Jesus as the new Moses. We will find Moses imagery throughout Matthew's Gospel.

At what point in Jesus's ministry did he cleanse the Temple? Matthew and Luke both present this scene near the end of Jesus's public ministry (Matt 21:12–17; Luke 19:45–46) while John has Jesus cleanse the Temple at the beginning of his ministry (John 2:14–16). The authors/editors are not claiming historical chronological order when they describe events. Rather, since oral tradition did not pass on exact chronology, they are free to order events as they see fit.

MATTHEW'S WRITTEN SOURCES

Although the Gospel according to Matthew appears first in the New Testament, Scripture scholars do not think that Matthew's Gospel was written first. Rather, evidence shows that Mark was the first of our canonical Gospels to take its present form, probably about 65 CE, and that Mark was a written source for both Matthew's (80 CE) and Luke's (85 CE) Gospels. A great deal of Mark is repeated in Matthew's and Luke's Gospels, although not always in the same order. If you removed from Matthew's and Luke's Gospels all that appears in Mark, Matthew and Luke still have a great deal of similar material, mostly sayings attributed to Jesus. Scripture scholars call this second written source Q, the first letter of the German word *quelle*, meaning *source*. In addition, the Gospels attributed to Matthew and Luke each have other sources, those in Matthew referred to as *M* and those in Luke referred to as *L*. Despite their common sources, each Gospel is unique primarily because each is addressed to a specific audience contemporary with the author/editor. As we will explore at great length, Matthew's Gospel was written for a primarily Jewish audience. That is one of the reasons that Matthew is constantly alluding to the Old Testament. Matthew is presenting Jesus as the fulfillment of all of God's covenant promises to the Israelites.

As we read Matthew's Gospel, we will see that this account of the good news is not a single literary form, such as an epistle, but includes a number of different literary forms: a genealogy, a birth narrative, call stories, parables, miracle stories, discourses, a passion narrative, and post-resurrection appearance stories. As we examine the Old Testament allusions, we will, of course, take into account the literary form being used. As stated before, if we misunderstand the literary form, we will misunderstand the intent of the author and therefore the revelation that the inspired author is teaching.

CANONICITY

So far, we have discussed four of the five steps that resulted in the Gospel according to Matthew, the steps of events, oral tradition, written tradition, and edited tradition. The fifth step is that some books eventually were embraced by the Church because they faithfully reflected the beliefs of the people and were used in worship and teaching. Such books are considered inspired. They truthfully reveal what God has chosen to reveal to God's people. These books comprise the New Testament and are called *canonical*. The root of the word *canon* is *reed*. A reed was used as a ruler to measure things. When a book is accepted as canonical, the Church is saying that this book is a true measure of our faith.

During the first few centuries of Christianity, the canon was in the process of being formed. Oral tradition grew into written tradition because of both geographic distance and the passage of time. Those who had originally witnessed the events surrounding Jesus and had passed on their knowledge through oral tradition were no longer living on earth. Connection to those first apostolic witnesses played an important role in the acceptance of certain books as canonical, including the Gospel according to Matthew. However, attributing a Gospel to an apostle is not claiming that the apostle personally wrote the Gospel. It is claiming that the apostle had a traditional relationship with the community that contributed to producing the Gospel.

One reason that the Gospel according to Matthew was attributed to Matthew, the apostle and tax collector (called Matthew in Matthew 9:9–13; called *Levi* in Mark 2:14–17 and Luke 5:27–32), is that a second-century bishop in Asia Minor, Papias, was reported by a fourth-century Church historian, Eusebius, to have said that Matthew had collected and published the sayings of Jesus in Hebrew. We simply do not know what relationship the apostle Matthew had to the Gospel, written in Greek Koine, that is now attributed to him.

Despite our knowledge of the process that resulted in the Gospel according to Matthew, when discussing the Gospel I will continue to refer to Matthew as the author or editor because of this traditional attribution and because of the title of this inspired canonical book, the Gospel according to Matthew.

WHY IS MATTHEW FIRST IN THE NEW TESTAMENT CANON?

Scripture scholars think that Matthew is first in the New Testament canon because the early Church fathers believed that Matthew's Gospel was the first to be written. As we have already discussed, that is no longer the majority opinion. However, there could not be a more appropriate first book in what Christians call the *New Testament* than the Gospel according to Matthew. Why?

To respond to this question, let us picture the social situation in which this Gospel was written. The author/editor of this Gospel was a Jew writing to Jews, most likely in Antioch, Syria, around 80 CE. He was both a faithful Jew and a faithful Christian. In the first century CE you could be both at the same time. However, belief in Jesus had caused division in the Jewish community. Some believed Jesus was the fulfillment of all of God's promises to the Israelites, as did the author of this Gospel, and some did not. Also, Gentiles had become Christians, and they did not follow all the Jewish laws regarding circumcision and eating restrictions. Could a faithful Jew be a Christian when Gentiles, unclean people, were also accepted as Christians?

The author of our first Gospel is teaching his fellow Jews that Jesus is the fulfillment of the promises that God made to their ancestors, especially to Abraham and David (the genealogy). Jesus embodies the history of the Jewish people (the birth narrative). Jesus is the new Moses who has authority from God to promulgate a new law (the Sermon on the Mount). Jesus fulfills the words of the prophets through the centuries (stated over and over). Each of these claims will be discussed further in future chapters.

Because the author of this Gospel is a faithful Jew and a faithful Christian, his work is a perfect bridge between the Old and New Testaments. The New Testament in no way has replaced what Christians call the Old Testament. Rather, the Old and New Testaments are part of one story, and knowledge of the Old Testament is absolutely necessary in order to understand the revelation that the inspired New Testament authors are teaching.

2

MATTHEW'S GENEALOGY

The Gospel according to Matthew begins with these words: "An account of the genealogy of Jesus the Messiah, the son of David, the son of Abraham" (Matt 1:1). Matthew then proceeds to sum up the whole history of Israel by dividing that history into three periods: from Abraham to David, from David to the Babylonian exile, and from the Babylonian exile to the birth of Jesus. So, in order to understand what this inspired author is teaching his contemporaries (and us), we will first give a short account of the history that undergirds not only the genealogy but all of Matthew's Old Testament allusions. We will then explore what Matthew is emphasizing in his unique account of Jesus's genealogy.

A HISTORICAL OVERVIEW

Matthew's genealogy does not start with Adam, as does Luke's. Rather, it starts with Abraham. Abraham is "the beginning of the story" when it comes to the salvation history that we read about in the Old Testament. Abraham lived about 1850 BCE. He had a profound religious experience that changed not only his life, and not only the lives of his physical descendants, but the lives of all people who have ever claimed to be Muslim, Jewish, or Christian. Abraham is the father in faith for all three of these world religions.

We read of Abraham's call in chapter 12 of the first book of the Bible, Genesis.

> Now the LORD said to Abraham, "Go from your country and your kindred and your father's house to the land that I will show you. I will make of you a great nation, and I will bless you, and make your name great, so that you will be a blessing. I will bless those who bless you, and the one who curses you I will curse; and in you all the families of the earth shall be blessed." (Gen 12:1–3)

Abraham obeyed the Lord, left his homeland, and went to Canaan. There the Lord made a covenant with Abraham.

> When Abram was ninety-nine years old, the LORD appeared to Abram and said to him, "I am God Almighty; walk before me, and be blameless. And I will make my covenant between me and you, and will make you exceedingly numerous." Then Abram fell on his face; and God said to him, "As for me, this is my covenant with you: You shall be the ancestor of a multitude of nations. No longer shall your name be Abram, but your name shall be Abraham; for I have made you the ancestor of a multitude of nations. I will make you exceedingly fruitful; and I will make nations of you, and kings shall come from you. I will establish my covenant between me and you, and your offspring after you throughout their generations, for an everlasting covenant, to be God to you and to your offspring after you." (Gen 17:1–7)

A covenant is an unbreakable bond that carries responsibilities on both sides. The English word *testament* is used to translate the Greek and Hebrew words for *covenant*. So, when we use the words *Old Testament* and *New Testament*, we are referring to the covenant God made with God's people. By beginning his genealogy with Abraham, Matthew is placing the story of "Jesus the Messiah" solidly in the context of God's covenant with Abraham and his descendants.

Matthew then names fourteen generations of ancestors of Jesus, ending this first section of his genealogy with King David. King David lived about 1000 BCE. The basic historic facts between Abraham (1850 BCE) and King David are these: Abraham's descendants lived in Canaan for four generations. Then, because of a famine, they moved to Egypt where they lived in slavery for four hundred years. Moses was called by God to lead the people out of slavery and back to the promised land. The exodus occurred around 1250 BCE.

Moses is not an ancestor of Jesus named in Matthew's genealogy. He was from the tribe of Levi (Exod 2:1), not the tribe of Judah. However, Moses is one of the most pivotal characters in the Old Testament. Moses was called to lead his people out of slavery and back to the land God promised to Abraham. Moses, too, had a deep spiritual experience of God's presence and guidance.

In the Book of Exodus, God gives Moses these instructions:

> Thus you shall say to the house of Jacob, and tell the Israelites: You have seen what I did to the Egyptians, and how I bore you on eagles' wings and brought you to myself. Now therefore, if you obey my voice and keep my covenant, you shall be my treasured possession out of all the peoples. Indeed, the whole earth is mine, but you shall be for me a priestly kingdom and a holy nation. These are the words that you shall speak to the Israelites. (Exod 19:3b–6)

Moses then receives the law on Mt. Sinai and delivers it to the people.

Knowledge of Moses is important because, as we will discuss later, the author of Matthew's Gospel presents Jesus as the new Moses who teaches a new law. This new law does not abolish the Law and the prophets; it fulfills them (Matt 5:17).

The period after the people return to Canaan is called the period of the judges. This two-hundred-year period starts with Joshua, Moses's companion and successor, and ends with Samuel, the bridge between the period of the judges, when the twelve tribes settled and lived in Canaan, and the beginning of kingship in Israel.

The twelve tribes who occupied the land of Canaan were the descendants of Jacob, Abraham's grandson. The twelve tribes constituted a loose federation. At times of threat from other nations, a leader would arise and lead the people to victory. These tribal leaders were called judges. Samuel was a judge of the eleventh century BCE, but he was also a prophet and a priest. Samuel anointed both Saul and David as the first and second kings of Israel.

David is the most famous king. He united the twelve tribes into one kingdom, he established Jerusalem as the capital of the kingdom, and he brought the ark of the covenant, God's dwelling place, to Jerusalem. We read of God's covenant with David in both 2 Samuel and in Psalms. In 2 Samuel, God directs the prophet Nathan to tell David:

> Thus says the Lord of hosts: I took you from the pasture, from following the sheep to be prince over my people Israel; and I have been with you wherever you went, and have cut off all your enemies from before you; and I will make for you a great name, like the name of the great ones of the earth.... When your days are fulfilled and you lie down with your ancestors, I will raise up your offspring after you, who shall come forth from your body, and I will establish his kingdom.... Your house and your kingdom shall be made secure forever before me; your throne shall be established forever. (2 Sam 7:8b–9, 12, 16)

God's covenant with David is also celebrated in Psalm 89. God says,

> I have made a covenant with my chosen one.
>   I have sworn to my servant David:
> "I will establish your descendants forever,
>   and build your throne for all generations."...
>   I have set the crown on one who is mighty,
>   I have exalted one chosen from the people.
> I have found my servant David;
>   with my holy oil I have anointed him....
> I will make him the firstborn,
>   the highest of the kings of the earth.

Forever I will keep my steadfast love for him,
  and my covenant with him will stand firm.
I will establish his line forever,
  and his throne as long as the heavens endure.
    (Ps 89:3–4, 19b–20, 27–29)

Next to Jesus, David is the most important person in Matthew's genealogy. (More about this later.)

The next historic period in Matthew's genealogy is the time between King David (1000 BCE) and the Babylonian exile (587–537 BCE). David's united kingdom, made up of the twelve tribes of Israel, lasted only until 922 BCE. For two hundred years there were two kingdoms: Israel, which included the ten northern tribes, and Judah, which included the two southern tribes. David's descendants continued to reign in Judah. The Northern Kingdom lasted until 721 BCE, when it was conquered by the Assyrians. The Southern Kingdom lasted until 587 BCE, when it was captured by the Babylonians. The Babylonians forced all the upper-class citizens to go into exile in Babylon.

The role of prophets in the united kingdom, and later in Israel and Judah, was, for the most part, coextensive with kingship. The word *prophet* means *one who speaks for another.* Some people were against Israel having a king because they feared that the people would forget that it is God who is king. It was the prophet's job to speak for God and to remind the king and the people who was really king. That is why a prophet's oracle often starts with the words, "Yahweh says…." The prophet is reminding the king and the people of their covenant relationship with God. If the people are suffering, the prophet offers hope because God is faithful, and God loves God's people. If the people are sinning, the prophet warns of future suffering and calls the people to repent. Matthew's Gospel will regularly say that Jesus's words and actions "fulfill the words of the prophets."

Matthew ends the second section of his genealogy with the words "at the time of the deportation to Babylon." The exile was a terrible time for the Israelites. They could not help but ask, "Where is God now? Are we still God's people? Is God still our God? Does the covenant even exist?" The last of the great prophets, who offered hope during these difficult times, lived immediately before, during, and shortly after the Babylonian exile (Jeremiah, Ezekiel, Third Isaiah [Isa 56—66], Haggai, and Zechariah [520 BCE]).

Some of the most beautiful prophesies of hope during this period are in the Book of Jeremiah. Jeremiah helped the people believe that God was still their God and they were still God's people, despite the fact that they no longer had their kingdom or their king. Jeremiah helped the people reinterpret the covenant so that it was centered more on one's personal relationship with God than on exterior things such as the kingdom and the king.

Jeremiah, on God's behalf, says:

> The days are surely coming, says the LORD, when I will make a new covenant with the house of Israel and the house of Judah. It will not be like the covenant that I made with their ancestors when I took them by the hand to bring them out of the land of Egypt—a covenant that they broke, though I was their husband, says the LORD. But this is the covenant that I will make with the house of Israel after those days, says the LORD: I will put my law within them, and I will write it on their hearts; and I will be their God, and they shall be my people. (Jer 31:31–33)

As we will soon see when we return to Matthew's Gospel, Jeremiah is laying the groundwork, the foundation, for a "new covenant," a New Testament, in which the covenant will not be about land or kingship and will not be limited to the Israelites. As God said to Abraham, the covenant will include "a multitude of nations," even Gentiles!

The exile ended in a most unexpected way. Cyrus, who was a Persian, conquered the Babylonians and allowed the Israelites to return home. Once back in Judah, the Israelites did not have self-rule except for a short time beginning in the second century BCE under the Maccabees (167–163 BCE). First, they lived under Persian rule. Then Alexander the Great conquered them (332 BCE) and they lived under Greek rule. In 63 BCE the Romans conquered them and so they were living under Roman rule at the time Jesus was born. The returned exiles were not led by judges, by kings, or by prophets. Rather, their leaders were priests who rebuilt the Temple and did a final editing of the peoples' inherited oral and written traditions about their covenant relationship with God. (The first connected narrative of the story of God's covenant relationship with Abraham's descendants was composed about the time of King David [1000 BCE]. However, the traditional accounts were edited, and added to, several times: once when the united kingdom split into Israel and Judah, again when the Northern Kingdom fell to the Assyrians, and again after the Babylonian exile, when the accounts that we read in what Christians call the *Old Testament* reached their final form.)

So, in Jesus's time, many of the Jewish people had returned to Judah, but they did not have their own kingdom, a kingdom they understood God to have promised them. They hoped, they even expected, that God would send them a messiah, an anointed one, through whom God's promises would once more be fulfilled. When Matthew begins his genealogy by saying, "An account of the genealogy of Jesus the Messiah, the son of David, the son of Abraham" (Matt 1:1), Matthew is claiming that Jesus is the fulfillment of all of God's promises to God's chosen people throughout the centuries.

This basic knowledge of the history of the Israelites will be very helpful to us as we examine Matthew's many allusions to the Old Testament. Knowledge of the historical contexts of the allusions will be a necessary tool as we probe just what Matthew is teaching his audience.

WHAT IS UNIQUE ABOUT MATTHEW'S GENEALOGY?

Matthew had Old Testament sources for his genealogy. Scripture scholars think that Matthew's main sources for the first two sections of fourteen generations of his genealogy were Genesis, Ruth, and 1 Chronicles. We do not know his sources for the third section of the fourteen generations from the Babylonian exile to Jesus's birth.

However, Matthew's genealogy is unique in several aspects. The first is the structure of the genealogy into three sections of fourteen generations each. This structure was obviously important to Matthew's purposes because he had to leave out some names in the second section of the genealogy so that he would have fourteen names. Also, even though Matthew says, "So all the generations from Abraham to David are fourteen generations; and from David to the deportation to Babylon, fourteen generations; and from the deportation to Babylon to the Messiah, fourteen generations" (Matt 1:17), Matthew includes only thirteen generations in the third section. What is so important about the number fourteen?

Scripture scholars surmise that Matthew is following a practice called *gematria.* In gematria a numerical value is assigned to the consonants of Hebrew words. The numerical value of the consonants in King David's name is fourteen. So, the very structure of the genealogy emphasizes David.

David is highlighted in Matthew's genealogy. He is named five times. When David was king, the Israelites believed that God's covenant promises to Abraham had been fulfilled. As history unfolded, as the kingdom divided and was conquered, the people began to question God's fidelity. They longed for a messiah. Matthew is proclaiming that Jesus is that longed-for king, that longed-for messiah. However, Jesus's kingship, Jesus's ministry, and Jesus's kingdom will be a sharp contrast to those of David.

Another unique aspect of Matthew's genealogy is that he includes five women, four by name. The women are Tamar, Rahab, Ruth, Uriah's wife, and Mary. Who are these women? We know that they were in the male line from Abraham to David to Joseph, but why does Matthew mention them in his genealogy?

Tamar, the mother of Perez, seduced her father-in-law, Judah, an ancestor of King David (see Gen 38). Tamar was the childless widow of Judah's son. According to law, she was to be given to her dead husband's brother so that she could bear a child. When this brother also died, Judah was unwilling to give her to his third son. So, Tamar disguised herself and seduced Judah. She became pregnant and gave birth to twins, "Perez and Zerah by Tamar" (Matt 1:3). Perez, too, was an ancestor of King David.

Rahab was a Canaanite prostitute who helped the Israelites conquer Jericho after they crossed the Red Sea and returned to the promised land (see Josh 2; 6:22–26). Rahab hid Israelite spies while they were preparing for battle. She then helped them escape in exchange for a promise that she and her whole family would be protected when the Israelites conquered the town. The Israelites were true to their promise and protected her whole family. Matthew tells us that Salmon was the "father of Boaz by Rahab" (Matt 1:5).

Ruth, too, was not an Israelite. She was a Moabite who lived during the time of the Judges (1200–1050 BCE). Ruth married an Israelite who died and left her a widow at a young age. Instead of returning to her own people, Ruth stayed with the Israelites. Naomi, Ruth's mother-in-law, encouraged her to return to the Moabites, but Ruth refused. She said:

> Do not press me to leave you
> or to turn back from following you!
> Where you go, I will go;
> Where you lodge, I will lodge.
> Your people shall be my people,
> and your God my God. (Ruth 1:16)

Ruth then met and married a kinsman of Naomi's named Boaz. They had a son named Obed. So, Ruth became David's great-grandmother (Ruth 4:13–17).

The fourth woman who appears in Matthew's genealogy is not named; she is referred to as "the wife of Uriah." Her name is Bathsheba. Bathsheba is the woman David saw bathing on a rooftop. He thought that she was very beautiful, had her brought to his house, and slept with her even though he knew she was the wife of one of his soldiers, Uriah, who was away at battle. When Bathsheba told David that she was pregnant, David tried to hide his adultery by bringing Uriah home from battle. However, Uriah did not go to his home and sleep with his wife, so David's ruse did not work. David then arranged for Uriah to be killed in battle. He then married Bathsheba, and she once more conceived a child who later became King Solomon (see 2 Sam 11—12:24).

The fifth woman in the genealogy, Jesus's mother, is named: Her name is Mary. Notice that Matthew breaks his pattern of naming fathers when he gets to Joseph and Mary. Rather than saying, "And Joseph was the father of Jesus," he says, "and Jacob the father of Joseph the husband of Mary, of whom Jesus was born, who is called Messiah" (Matt 1:16). We will understand this strange wording when we read the next few paragraphs of Matthew's Gospel, the annunciation to Joseph.

Why does Matthew break convention and include these particular women in his genealogy? One theory is that Matthew knew that some in his audience had trouble believing that Mary's son could possibly be the Messiah because Mary was known to have been with child before Joseph and she lived together. They thought that she obviously lacked virtue. Perhaps Matthew was pointing out that Mary wasn't the only woman in the blood line of the Messiah who could have been the object of prejudice by her contemporaries: some for lack of virtue (Tamar, Rahab, Bathsheba) and some for being foreigners (Rahab, Ruth), or both. Still, God, in God's providence, allowed these women to be God's instruments in fulfilling God's covenant promises to God's people.

One more question needs to be addressed regarding Matthew's genealogy: If Matthew is not claiming that Joseph is Jesus's biological father, why give us Joseph's genealogy? Why does Joseph's genealogy have any relevance? The answer to this question is that by taking Mary into his home, by naming Jesus, and by raising him, Joseph became Jesus's legal father, and Jesus became Joseph's legal son. According to Jewish custom, Jesus would have all the rights of a biological son.

Matthew ends his genealogy by once more claiming that Jesus is the Messiah (Matt 1:16b), the same claim made as the genealogy began (Matt 1:1). Matthew, throughout his Gospel, will support this claim. Jesus, the Messiah, is the fulfillment of God's covenant promises to God's people.

3

MATTHEW'S INFANCY NARRATIVES

Immediately after his genealogy, Matthew tells us several stories surrounding Jesus's birth. Such stories are called *infancy narratives.* Two of our four Gospels include infancy narratives: the Gospels according to Matthew and Luke. The two accounts agree on the core of the story: In both accounts, Mary conceives Jesus through the Holy Spirit before she lives with Joseph. An angel directs that the child should be named Jesus and says that Jesus will be a savior. Jesus is born in Bethlehem at the time of Herod the Great. However, the stories differ on many plot elements. Only in Matthew do we read about the star, the magi, the massacre of the children in Bethlehem, and the flight into Egypt. Only in Luke do we read that Jesus is born in a manger, that his birth is announced to shepherds, and that the shepherds go to Bethlehem and find Jesus lying in the manger. Why are the stories so different? The answer to this question lies in understanding the literary form of *infancy narrative.*

WHAT IS AN INFANCY NARRATIVE?

The infancy narratives were the last of the stories to develop in the oral traditions surrounding Jesus's birth. Imagine that you and I lived during Jesus's public ministry, that we were his disciples, and that we were devastated by his crucifixion because we had believed that he was the Messiah, and that he would reestablish self-rule in the renewed kingdom of Israel. But, instead of freeing us from Roman rule, Jesus was killed by the Romans. All hope was lost. Then, we experienced Jesus as once more alive! Jesus had risen from the dead! When, full of joy and excitement, we shared this good news, we would not have started by saying, "Did you hear about the baby born in Bethlehem?" We would have proclaimed, "Jesus has risen! Jesus appeared to me, and I know he is alive!" So, the earliest oral traditions to develop were narratives about the passion, death, and resurrection.

If you were a disciple of Jesus who had experienced his presence after his resurrection and had told me of your experience, I might well have asked you, "Did Jesus do anything when he was alive that made you think he would do this after he died?" Your answer might well have been, "Actually, he did. He performed many miracles. There is that blind person who can now see. There is that deaf person who can now hear. Lepers were cured. He even raised up a child who we all thought had died. Jesus worked many miracles during his public ministry." So, the second body of material that developed in oral tradition was a collection of miracle stories.

The first Christians were Jewish. On the Sabbath, which began at sundown on Friday and ended at sundown on Saturday, they were accustomed to gathering in synagogues and reading Scripture, what Christians now call the Old Testament. In addition, on Sundays they started to gather in one another's homes to celebrate the Eucharist. Over time, Jesus's followers wanted to know more about what Jesus said. So, oral tradition developed collections of Jesus's sayings.

The last stories to develop in oral tradition were the stories about Jesus's birth. Infancy narratives already existed in the culture. The function of an infancy narrative was not to respond to the request, "Tell me exactly what happened." Rather, this literary form responds to the request, "Tell me how great this person became as you know from hindsight." The infancy narratives explain the identity of Jesus Christ as it was understood in the light of the resurrection.

As we have already mentioned, the birth narratives agree on the core historical facts: The time in history when Jesus was born. The geographical location of Jesus's birth. The political rulers at the time. That Jesus's mother was Mary, and that Joseph took Jesus into his home and raised him as his own son. They also agree on the theological claims: Jesus is God's own son, God with us, who has saved the human race from our sins.

However, as we have also already noted, the stories do not agree on plot elements such as the star, the Magi, the manger, and the shepherds. The reason for this is that the stories employ a literary device called *midrash*. In midrash, the author introduces plot elements into the story that are allusions to Old Testament texts. The allusions reveal the significance of the core historical events as they were understood in hindsight. In order to understand what the story teaches about the events, one has to recognize the Old Testament allusions. With this knowledge regarding the literary form of *infancy narrative* firmly in mind, we will now examine the stories Matthew tells us surrounding the birth of Jesus Christ.

THE ANNUNCIATION TO JOSEPH

When we hear the word *annunciation*, our minds probably go first to the Angel Gabriel's announcement of Jesus's birth to Mary (see Luke 1:26–38). Unlike Luke, Matthew does not tell us that story. In Matthew, the annunciation is to Joseph (see Matt 1:18–25). By having the annunciation be to Joseph, Matthew clearly connects this story to his genealogy. The child announced to Joseph is going to be the fulfillment of the promises God made to Abraham and to David.

First, Matthew sets the scene: Joseph and Mary are engaged but have not yet lived together. Mary is "with child from the Holy Spirit" (Matt 1:18). Notice that Matthew tells the reader this astounding fact before the angel tells Joseph that the child whom Mary has conceived is "from the Holy Spirit" (Matt 1:20). Before hearing this from the angel, Joseph had planned to dismiss Mary quietly. In other words, he was going to act in obedience to the Law as it is spelled out in Deuteronomy 22:13–30. Joseph had no way of knowing if Mary was at fault. If she willingly had sex with another man, she should be stoned to death. If she was raped, she is not at fault. Joseph does not presume the worst and does not want to publicly disgrace her.

Notice that the angel addresses Joseph as "son of David" (Matt 1:20). In other words, Joseph is being reminded that he is of the messianic line, and so will be the child in Mary's womb if Joseph obeys the angel and takes Mary and the child into his home. Joseph is then told, "You are to name him Jesus, for he will save his people from their sins" (Matt 1:21). The word *Jesus* means *Savior* or *God saves*.

The Jews living under Roman rule were expecting a savior, a Christ, a messiah. (Both *Christ* and *messiah* mean *an anointed one*. *Christ* is the Greek form of the word *messiah*. Kings, prophets, and priests were all anointed.) But the savior the people were expecting was a person who would free them from Roman rule. The expectation was not that the savior would save his people from their sins. However, there is a connection between the two ideas because the prophets taught that the Israelites suffered exile in Babylon due to their sin, to their lack of being faithful to their covenant relationship with God. If the people were saved from their sin, they might also be saved from the ramifications of their sin. They might once more have their king and their kingdom, as they did under David.

Matthew then says, "All this took place to fulfill what had been spoken by the Lord through the prophet: 'Look, the virgin shall conceive and bear a son, and they shall name him Emmanuel,' which means, 'God is with us'" (Matt 1:23). This is the first of Matthew's fulfillment citations. Matthew quotes Old Testament passages and reinterprets them in a new context so that they take on a new meaning in the light of events.

The passage that Matthew quotes is from Isaiah 7:14. This passage from Isaiah dates to the time when the Northern Kingdom, Israel, and the Southern Kingdom, Judah, were divided. Israel was being threatened by Assyria and wanted Ahaz, the king of Judah, to join in fighting off the threat. Ahaz thought it might be better to pay tribute to Assyria and buy protection than to join the Northern Kingdom in fighting Assyria (732 BCE). The prophet at the time was Isaiah. It was the prophet's role to call the people to fidelity to their covenant with God. Isaiah warned Ahaz that he should not place his trust in political alliances. He should place his trust in God.

Isaiah tells King Ahaz that God will give him a sign of God's presence and protection. "Hear then O house of David!...Therefore the

Lord himself will give you a sign. Look, the young woman is with child and shall bear a son, and shall name him Immanuel" (Isa 7:13a, 14). Isaiah is reminding Ahaz that God has made promises to the house of David that God will keep. "A young woman," presumably Ahaz's wife, Abijah, is with child. The Davidic line will continue. Ahaz does not have to sell out to the Assyrians. Abijah did bear the future king, King Hezekiah. According to 2 Kings 18, Hezekiah was not a weak king like his father. The narrator of 2 Kings considers Hezekiah second only to David as a good king.

The passage Matthew quotes from Isaiah did not foretell Mary's conceiving Jesus through the Holy Spirit. However, by quoting it, Matthew does tell his readers that, through Mary's child, God's covenant promises to the Davidic line are being fulfilled. The passage is "fulfilled," not in the sense of a prognostication coming true, but in the sense of the words taking on a whole new level of meaning in the light of new events. The young woman is now understood to be Mary, not Abijah. The son is now understood to be Jesus, not Hezekiah.

That the young woman's child will be named *Emmanuel* is also very important. *Emmanuel* means *God with us.* "God with us" is a reference to covenant love. God promised that he was the Israelites' God, and they were God's people. With the loss of country, exile in Babylon, and return to Judah only to be ruled, for the most part, by foreign nations, the people could not help but ask if God was still with them and if they were still God's people. *Emmanuel* answers that question. God is still with God's people. However, God is with God's people in a way far beyond what anyone had understood before. When Matthew claims that Mary conceived Jesus through the Holy Spirit, he is claiming the *incarnation.* Through Jesus, God is with his people in an even more intimate relationship than was understood before. John's Gospel probes this same mystery with the words "And the Word became flesh and lived among us" (John 1:14).

The story of the annunciation to Joseph ends with Matthew telling his Jewish audience, and us, that Joseph named Mary's child, and now his child, *Jesus.* Jesus, who, from Matthew's point of view (around 80 CE), saved his people from their sins. Jesus, who fulfilled all of God's promises to Abraham and David. Jesus, whom Matthew claims as the Messiah in the opening sentence of his Gospel: "An account of the genealogy of

Jesus the Messiah" (Matt 1:1). However, as the story continues, Jesus will be a very different kind of messiah from what many expected, and Jesus's kingdom will be a very different kingdom from that over which King David reigned.

THE VISIT OF THE WISE MEN

Matthew's next infancy narrative is the story of the wise men from the East who come seeking Jesus, bearing gifts. Matthew tells us that the wise men go to Jerusalem and ask King Herod, "Where is the child who has been born king of the Jews? For we observed his star at its rising, and have come to pay him homage" (Matt 2:2). King Herod the Great is a historical figure. He was a vassal king appointed by the Roman emperor and was known to hold viciously on to his power (ruled 37 BCE–4 BCE). Obviously, Herod wants to remain king of the Jews.

The story, as it continues, employs midrash to teach what was understood about Jesus after his resurrection. That is, Matthew interweaves historical characters (Jesus, Mary, Joseph, Herod) with plot elements (the star, the wise men) that are allusions to Old Testament texts. By quoting and alluding to Old Testament passages, Matthew is once more assuring his primarily Jewish audience that Jesus is the promised messiah despite being different from their expectations.

The visiting wise men who follow a star and bring gifts to the newborn king are allusions to two Old Testament passages, one from Numbers and one from Isaiah.

The passage from Numbers is:

> I see him, but not now;
> I behold him, but not near—
> A star shall come out of Jacob,
> And a scepter shall rise out of Israel. (Num 24:17)

The historical setting for this passage is the time after the Israelites' exodus from slavery in Egypt (1250 BCE) and as they are preparing to conquer the promised land. The Israelites are camped on the plains of Moab across the Jordan from Jericho. The speaker, the "I" in the passage, is

Balaam. He has been asked by the king of Moab, Balak, to curse the Israelites. Balaam refuses to do that, but rather blesses the Israelites. Balaam believes that it is God's will that the Israelites become victorious over their enemies and conquer the land. This will happen because a "star," a great leader for the Israelites, will arise in the future.

While the setting of the quotation is before the Israelites conquered the promised land, the time of the final editing of the story is much later, after the Babylonian exile (587–537 BCE), when the priests were going over their inherited oral and written traditions and putting them into their final form, our Old Testament. The "star that will come out of Jacob" and the "scepter that will rise out of Israel" were both understood, in hindsight, to be references to King David (1000 BCE), through whom the hope offered in Balaam's oracle was understood to have been fulfilled. Matthew reinterprets the "star" as an actual, physical star, and combines this interpretation with a passage from the Book of Isaiah:

> Arise, shine; for your light has come,
> and the glory of the Lord has risen upon you.
> For darkness shall cover the earth
> and thick darkness the peoples;
> but the Lord will arise upon you,
> and his glory will appear over you.
> Nations shall come to your light,
> and kings to the brightness of your dawn....
>
> I will make you majestic forever,
> a joy from age to age.
> You shall suck the milk of nations,
> you shall suck the breast of kings;
> And you shall know that I the Lord am your savior
> and your Redeemer, the Mighty One of Jacob.
>
> Instead of bronze I will bring gold,
> instead of iron I will bring silver;
> Instead of wood, bronze,
> instead of stones, iron.

I will appoint Peace as your overseer
and Righteousness as your taskmaster. (Isa 60:1–3, 15b–17)

This passage is set during the Babylonian exile. The prophet is comforting the exiles and assuring them that God is still their God. God will free them from exile and bring them back to Judah. Not only will their nation be restored, but other nations will bow before them. By picturing wise men from the East seeking out the infant Jesus, "the King of the Jews," and bearing gifts, Matthew is teaching that the hope Isaiah was offering the exiles has been fulfilled in Jesus Christ.

In order to answer the wise men's question, "Where is the child who has been born King of the Jews?" (Matt 2:2), Herod asks all the chief priests and scribes where the messiah is to be born. Their response is, "In Bethlehem of Judea; for so it has been written by the prophet: 'And you, Bethlehem, in the land of Judah, are by no means least among the rulers of Judah; for from you shall come a ruler who is to shepherd my people Israel'" (Matt 2:5–6). Matthew is once more alluding to two Old Testament passages from Micah and 2 Samuel.

In the Book of Micah, we read: "But you, O Bethlehem of Ephrathah, who are one of the little clans of Judah, from you shall come forth for me one who is to rule in Israel" (Mic 5:2). The historical setting for Micah's prophetical words is around 725 BCE. The Northern Kingdom (Israel) and the Southern Kingdom (Judah) have been divided since 922 BCE. Micah is preaching to both Israel and Judah, which are both being threatened by Assyria. Micah is warning the people that unless they repent and live in fidelity to covenant love, they will be conquered. Micah, known as a prophet of justice, reminds the people what the Lord requires of them: They must "do justice, love kindness, and walk humbly" with their God (Mic 6:8). At the same time, Micah preaches hope. God will remain faithful to God's covenant with God's people. In the future, another good king will come forth from Bethlehem, David's hometown. By alluding to this passage, Matthew confirms that Jesus is the fulfillment of Micah's prophecy of hope.

In addition to Micah, Matthew is alluding to 2 Samuel. In 2 Samuel we read: "Then all the tribes of Israel came to David at Hebron, and said…'The Lord said to you: It is you who shall be shepherd of my people Israel, you who shall be ruler over Israel'" (2 Sam 5:1a, 2b). David was then anointed king (1000 BCE). David succeeded in uniting the twelve tribes of Israel and reigned over the united kingdom for thirty-three years.

So, when Matthew pictures all the chief priests and scribes telling Herod that the king of the Jews who would shepherd God's people was to be born in Bethlehem, Matthew pictures them alluding to two Old Testament passages that were originally understood to refer to King David. As in the genealogy, by centering our attention on David, Matthew teaches that, in the light of the resurrection, Jesus is now understood to be the Son of David, the person through whom God has fulfilled God's promises to Abraham, to David, and to all the Israelites.

Following King Herod's instructions, the wise men follow the star to Bethlehem. They enter Jesus's house and find Jesus with his mother, Mary. The wise men kneel down, pay homage to Jesus, and offer him gifts of gold, frankincense, and myrrh. Matthew does not tell us the significance of the gifts. Later tradition understood the gold to symbolize kingship, the incense to symbolize divinity, and the myrrh to symbolize Jesus's redemptive suffering. Because there were three gifts, the wise men, symbolizing all nations coming and paying homage to Jesus, are traditionally referred to as the three kings.

THE ESCAPE TO EGYPT AND THE MASSACRE OF THE INNOCENTS

As the story continues, an angel once more appears to Joseph in a dream and warns him to flee to Egypt with Jesus and Mary because Herod wants to find and kill this "king of the Jews." Once more, Joseph obeys. Joseph, Mary, and Jesus flee to Egypt where they remain until Herod dies. Matthew then tells us, "This was to fulfill what had been spoken by the Lord through the prophet, 'Out of Egypt I have called my son'" (Matt 2:15).

In this passage Matthew is alluding to the prophet Hosea. The historical setting for the Book of Hosea is the Northern Kingdom in the eighth century BCE before the Northern Kingdom was conquered by the Assyrians (721 BCE). Hosea is teaching the Israelites about God's faithful love in the face of the people's unfaithfulness. He says:

> When Israel was a child, I loved him,
> and out of Egypt I called my son.
> The more I called them,
> the more they went from me;
> they kept sacrificing to the Baals,
> and offering incense to idols. (Hos 11:1–2)

Hosea is reminding the people that God, through Moses's leadership, freed the people from slavery in Egypt (1250 BCE). The son in the original prophecy is a personification of all the Israelites. However, in the light of Matthew's claims that Jesus was conceived through the Holy Spirit, the word *son* takes on a new meaning. Jesus is God's son in a completely new and different way.

Also, by referring to the exodus, Matthew is reminding his Jewish audience that Joseph, Jesus's father, was not the first Joseph who ended up in Egypt and saved his family by being there. In Genesis (see Gen 37—50) we read of Joseph, the son of Jacob and Rachel, who was sold into slavery by his jealous brothers. Joseph was taken to Egypt and sold again to an officer of the Pharoah. Joseph ended up being trusted by the Pharoah and having considerable authority. Years later, during a famine, his brothers came to Egypt seeking food. Joseph finally revealed his identity to his brothers, forgave them for selling him, and invited the whole family to come to Egypt and live with him.

Matthew then tells us that Herod was so infuriated that the wise men had not returned to him and told him where to find Jesus that he had all the male children in and around Bethlehem who were two or younger killed. Matthew then says,

> Then was fulfilled what had been spoken through the prophet Jeremiah:
> "A voice was heard in Ramah
> wailing and loud lamentation,

Rachel weeping for her children;
she refused to be consoled, because they are no more."
(Matt 2:17–18)

The passage Matthew quotes from Jeremiah expresses the profound grief people experience when their children die. Jeremiah lived during the time of the Babylonian exile. In this passage he names the terrible grief and suffering that the Israelites were experiencing in exile. At the same time, he assures the exiles that God is faithful to God's covenant promises, and that the exiles will return. Jeremiah says:

Thus says the LORD:
A voice is heard in Ramah,
lamentation and bitter weeping.
Rachel is weeping for her children;
she refuses to be comforted for her children,
because they are no more.
Thus says the LORD:
Keep your voice from weeping,
and your eyes from tears;
for there is a reward for your work,
says the LORD:
they shall come back from the land of the enemy;
there is hope for your future,
says the LORD:
your children will come back to their own country.
(Jer 31:15–17)

Rachel was a matriarch of the tribes in the Northern Kingdom because she was the mother of two of Jacob's sons, Joseph and Benjamin (see Gen 29—35). So, Rachel's "children" are the tribes of Israel. Jeremiah uses the long dead matriarch as a personification of national grief—the grief that all experienced when Assyria conquered the Northern Kingdom (ten tribes; 721 BCE) and when the Babylonians conquered the Southern Kingdom (two tribes) and forced all the upper-class citizens of Judah into exile (587–537 BCE). By quoting Jeremiah, Matthew adopts

Jeremiah's personification of Rachel as a symbol of profound, widespread grief.

In addition to recalling the passage from Jeremiah, Herod's slaughter of innocent babies would have immediately reminded Matthew's Jewish audience of the slaughter of the male babies at the time of Moses's birth (see Exod 1:15—2:10). Pharoah, the king of Egypt, ordered that all Hebrew male babies be killed by throwing them into the Nile River. Moses's mother hid him immediately after his birth. When she could hide him no more, she put him in a basket on the river's edge where the Pharoah's daughter found him. The Pharoah's daughter hired Moses's mother to nurse the baby and later took Moses as her son. As we will see, Moses imagery will continue as a kind of background music as we read Matthew's Gospel about Jesus.

Matthew ends his infancy narratives by reporting that after Herod died, Joseph, once more in obedience to an angel, moved his family out of Egypt. However, knowing that Jesus would still be in danger in Bethlehem, Joseph moved the family to Galilee. That is why Jesus was raised in Nazareth. Matthew then, for the fifth time in his infancy narratives, includes a fulfillment citation: "There he made his home in a town called Nazareth, so that what had been spoken through the prophets might be fulfilled, 'He will be called a Nazorean'" (Matt 2:23). Scripture scholars debate what Matthew wants to say by including this quotation. Matthew does not tell us the source of his quotation, but simply refers to "the prophets."

One suggestion is that Matthew is associating Jesus with a "Nazirite," such as Samson (see Judg 13:5–7) and Samuel (see 1 Sam 1:11). A Nazirite was a person consecrated to God whose ministry was to call others to commit themselves to God. In some instances, the vow to be a Nazirite was made by the child's parents. Some Nazirite vows were lifelong. More often the vows were for a specified amount of time. The Nazirites made three vows: not to drink wine or alcoholic beverages, not to cut their hair, and not to touch a corpse.

If Matthew is referring to a Nazirite in his quotation from the prophets, he is once more reinterpreting the prophets' words. Unlike a Nazirite, Jesus did not promise to drink no "fruit of the vine." Jesus was not, in any way, a person set apart. Rather, he drank wine, had dinner with sinners, and touched a corpse when he raised a dead person to new life.

Perhaps, if Matthew was making an allusion to Nazirites, he was doing it in order to make a contrast. Matthew has done this throughout his first two chapters. Jesus is a "son of David," but a very different kind of king, with a very different kingdom, from King David. Jesus is "Son of God," but those words take on an entirely different meaning in light of the incarnation. Jesus is the Messiah, but not at all what the people expected.

Imagine that you were a faithful Jew, part of Matthew's audience, in 80 CE. You want to continue to be a faithful Jew. Is becoming a disciple of Jesus Christ being a faithful Jew, or is it turning your back on two thousand years of a covenant relationship with God? Jews believe that there is only one God. Is believing that Jesus is God incarnate faithful to monotheism? Gentiles are becoming followers of Jesus and are not having to obey all of the Jewish dietary laws. Eucharist is being celebrated in home churches. Would joining Gentiles to celebrate Eucharist in each other's homes constitute being unfaithful to Jewish law?

In Matthew's genealogy and in his infancy narratives, Matthew is responding to these questions. Becoming a disciple of Jesus Christ is not turning your back on your covenant relationship with God. Rather, it is remaining faithful to it. "Jesus, the Messiah, the son of David" (Matt 1:1) is the fulfillment of all of God's promises to God's people. Through allusions to the Old Testament, the whole history of the Jewish people is included in Jesus's story: the promise to Abraham that in him "all the families of the earth will be blessed" (Gen 12:3b); Joseph's being sold to the Pharoah; Moses leading the people out of slavery in Egypt and preparing them to enter Canaan; the time of a united kingdom under King David; the terrible grief when the Northern Kingdom was conquered by the Assyrians, and the heartache when the Southern Kingdom was conquered by the Babylonians; the hope that God was still with them and that they were still God's people even while they were in exile; the return to Judah, but not under self-rule. By his allusions, Matthew teaches his Jewish audience that their whole salvation history has been fulfilled in Jesus Christ. Fidelity to Jesus Christ is fidelity to their covenant relationship with God.

4

THE BEGINNING OF JESUS'S PUBLIC MINISTRY

Between his infancy narratives and his passion narrative, Matthew divides his stories about Jesus's public ministry into five sections, each consisting of stories about Jesus and a sermon by Jesus. The first of these sections (Matt 3:1—7:29) begins by introducing us to John the Baptist and ends with the Sermon on the Mount. As we will see, an understanding of Old Testament allusions continues to be necessary in order to comprehend the inspired author's teaching.

JOHN THE BAPTIST

Matthew tells us that John the Baptist

> appeared in the wilderness of Judea, proclaiming, "Repent, for the kingdom of heaven has come near." This is the one of whom the prophet Isaiah spoke when he said,
>
> "The voice of one crying out in the wilderness:
> 'Prepare the way of the Lord,
> make his paths straight.'" (Matt 3:1–3)

In this passage, Matthew is claiming that John the Baptist is fulfilling the prophecy in Isaiah 40:3. Remember, Matthew is not claiming that a prognostication has come true. Rather, Matthew is claiming that, in the light of subsequent events, the words of the prophet have taken on a whole new level of meaning.

The historical setting for Isaiah 40:3 is just as the Babylonian exile was ending (537 BCE). Isaiah is offering comfort to the exiles, assuring them that their time of exile is over and that they can return to Judah. While historically the Babylonian exile ended because Cyrus, a Persian, conquered the Babylonians and allowed the Israelites to return home, Isaiah attributes this marvelous turn of events to God. God will lead God's people home.

So, when Isaiah says,

> A voice cries out:
> "In the wilderness prepare the way of the LORD,
> make straight in the desert a highway for our God," (Isa 40:3)

the "LORD" to whom Isaiah is referring is God. When Matthew applies these words to the role of John the Baptist, the "Lord" to whom John the Baptist is referring is Jesus. Once more, Matthew is telling his Jewish audience that Jesus is God's own son. Jesus is the Lord.

The words on John the Baptist's lips, "Repent, for the kingdom of heaven has come near" (Matt 3:1), are the exact same words with which Matthew pictures Jesus beginning his public ministry: "Jesus began to proclaim, 'Repent, for the kingdom of heaven has come near'" (Matt 4:17). The coming of the kingdom will be central to Jesus's preaching. In fact, the *kingdom* will be the central theme of the third of Matthew's five narrative/sermon sections (Matt 11:2—13:52). So, we will discuss what Jesus teaches about the *kingdom* in a future chapter. For now, let us say that both John the Baptist and Jesus use the word *kingdom* to refer to an entirely different reality from that referred to by those who spoke of the kingdom under David. Jesus's kingdom will not be a geopolitical kingdom but a spiritual, eternal kingdom.

Matthew tells us that "John wore clothing of camel's hair with a leather belt around his waist" (Matt 3:4). This is a subtle reference to the prophet Elijah. Elijah was a prophet in the Northern Kingdom of Israel who was a champion of monotheism. He denounced King Ahaziah (ruled 853–852 BCE) for being unfaithful to Israel's God. The king's messengers told the king of Elijah's judgment against him, and the king asked who this person was. They described Elijah as "a hairy man, with a leather belt around his waist" (2 Kings 1:8). The author of 2 Kings goes on to describe Elijah as ascending into heaven in a fiery chariot (2 Kings 2:11).

Because the story of Elijah pictured him as not dying but ascending to heaven in the fiery chariot, he was expected to return in preparation for God's establishing his kingdom on earth. The prophet Malachi says, "Lo, I will send you the prophet Elijah before the great and terrible day of the LORD comes. He will turn the hearts of parents to their children, and the hearts of children to their parents, so that I will not come and strike the land with a curse" (Mal 4:5–6).

Elijah's name also became associated with another passage in Malachi:

> See, I am sending my messenger to prepare the way before me, and the Lord whom you seek will suddenly come to his temple. The messenger of the covenant in whom you delight—indeed, he is coming, says the LORD of hosts. (Mal 3:1)

The Book of Malachi dates to the mid-fifth century BCE. The prophet is speaking to the returned exiles who are living in Jerusalem after the Babylonian exile. The author is reassuring the exiles that God still loves them and that their covenant relationship is still intact. The Book of Malachi is the last book in the Old Testament, and the words about Elijah being sent before the Lord comes (Mal 4:5–6) are the last words in the Old Testament. The stage is set for John the Baptist preparing the way of the Lord, Jesus Christ. The next book in the Bible is the Gospel according to Matthew.

DO NOT PRESUME

John the Baptist was a fiery preacher who called for repentance. He challenged the Pharisees and Sadducees, Jewish religious leaders who were coming to be baptized, not to presume their own superiority because they are children of Abraham. John says, "You brood of vipers!

Who warned you to flee from the wrath to come? Bear fruit worthy of repentance. Do not presume to say to yourselves, 'We have Abraham as our ancestor'; for I tell you, God is able from these stones to raise up children to Abraham" (Matt 3:7–9). With these words Matthew foreshadows that the kingdom will not be limited to the Jewish people.

THE BAPTISM OF JESUS

When Jesus comes to John and asks to be baptized, John objects. He humbly claims that rather than his baptizing Jesus, Jesus should baptize him. However, when Jesus persists, John acquiesces.

After Jesus's baptism, Matthew tells us that "the heavens opened to him and he saw the Spirit of God descending like a dove and alighting on him" (Matt 3:16). The idea of the heavens being open and God revealing God's self is not new in Scripture. In the Book of Isaiah, we read that Isaiah prayed, "O that you would tear open the heavens and come down" (Isa 64:1). The prophet Ezekiel claims that as he was with the exiles, "the heavens were opened, and I saw visions of God" (Ezek 1:1b).

In addition, Scripture scholars suggest that the description of the Spirit of God descending is an allusion to the very first verse in the Bible, Genesis 1:1, when God's Spirit (God's *breath* in some translations) hovers over the waters. God then speaks, "Let there be…" and creates all that exists.

In Matthew's Gospel the voice from heaven says, "This is my Son, the Beloved, with whom I am well pleased" (Matt 3:17). These words, too, are alluding to Old Testament passages. In Psalm 2, God is described as promising to establish Zion's king and says,

> You are my son;
>   today I have begotten you.
> Ask of me, and I will make the nations your heritage,
>   and the ends of the earth your possession. (Ps 2:7–8)

Also, the prophet Isaiah speaks of a suffering servant who will be a light to the nations. He says,

Here is my servant, whom I uphold.
    My chosen, in whom my soul delights;
I have put my spirit upon him;
    he will bring forth justice to the nations. (Isa 42:1)

What is Matthew conveying to his Jewish contemporaries, people who want to remain faithful to their two-thousand-year covenant with God, by alluding to these Old Testament texts? Matthew is once more explaining the identity of Jesus. Jesus is God's own son. Jesus will teach justice. Nations will receive Jesus's teaching. Through God's Spirit, who is always with Jesus, a new creation is beginning.

THE TEMPTATION IN THE DESERT

Matthew's account of Jesus's temptation in the desert is full of allusions to Old Testament texts. Shakespeare was not the first to understand that the devil can quote Scripture to suit his purpose. In Matthew's Gospel, in the dialogue between Jesus and the devil, both are quoting passages from the Old Testament, Jesus from the Book of Deuteronomy and the devil from Psalm 91.

The word *Deuteronomy* means *second law*. The setting for the Book of Deuteronomy is just as the Israelites are entering Canaan after their exodus from Egypt (1250 BCE) and their forty years in the desert. Moses is pictured as giving sermons that instruct the people about how they are to live in fidelity to covenant love when they enter the promised land. However, the time of the authors is not the same as the time of the setting. The final revision of Deuteronomy dates to the end of the Babylonian exile (537 BCE). Deuteronomy is addressed to those who had lived in exile but are now returning to live in Judah. The people are being taught to "love the LORD your God with all your heart, and with all your soul, and with all your might" (Deut 6:5).

Matthew begins the story of Jesus's temptation by saying that Jesus was in the wilderness and had fasted for forty days and forty nights. This, of course, would remind Matthew's audience of their ancestors' forty years in the desert. The theme of the story is that Jesus, who is the Son of God, will not abuse his authority to serve himself rather than to serve God's people and do God's will.

The devil begins the first two temptations by saying, "If you are the Son of God" (Matt 4:3, 6). The reader knows that Jesus is the Son of God. Matthew has already firmly established that fact in his genealogy and in his birth narratives. The devil is tempting Jesus to abuse his power to serve himself, not to serve God's people and reveal God's love to them. Knowing that Jesus is famished after fasting for forty days, the devil first tempts Jesus to feed himself by turning stones into bread. Jesus responds, "It is written, 'One does not live by bread alone, but by every word that comes from the mouth of God'" (Matt 4:4). Here Jesus is quoting Moses's instructions to the Israelites before they enter the promised land. Moses reminds the people that the Lord "humbled you by letting you hunger, then by feeding you with manna, with which neither you nor your ancestors were acquainted, in order to make you understand that one does not live by bread alone, but by every word that comes from the mouth of the LORD" (Deut 8:3).

With the second temptation, the devil, too, quotes Scripture, saying,

> "If you are the Son of God, throw yourself down; for it is written,
> 'He will command his angels concerning you,'
> and 'On their hands they will bear you up,
> so that you will not dash your foot against a stone.'" (Matt 4:6)

The devil tempts Jesus to abuse his power by making a spectacle of himself, a spectacle that is not in service to others, but is simply to prove his own identity. In offering this temptation, the devil accurately quotes Psalm 91, a psalm that assures God's people of God's protection. The psalm says,

> For he will command his angels concerning you
> to guard you in all your ways.
> On their hands they will bear you up,
> so that you will not dash your foot against a stone.
> (Ps 91:11–12)

Jesus responds by once more quoting Deuteronomy. Jesus says, "Again it is written, 'Do not put the Lord your God to the test'" (Matt 4:7). This quotation, too, is part of the instructions that Moses gave to the Israelites as they were preparing to enter the promised land. Moses says,

> Do not put the LORD your God to the test, as you tested him at Massah. You must diligently keep the commandments of the LORD your God, and his decrees, and his statutes that he has commanded you. Do what is right and good in the sight of the LORD, so that it may go well with you, and so that you may go in and occupy the good land that the LORD swore to your ancestors to give you. (Deut 6:16–18)

Since Jesus did not succumb to the temptation to abuse his power by serving himself or by making an amazing show of his power to no purpose, the devil tempts Jesus by offering him political power. All Jesus has to do is to worship the devil. After showing him the kingdoms of the world, the devil says, "All these I will give you, if you will fall down and worship me" (Matt 4:9). For a third time, Jesus quotes Deuteronomy. Jesus says, "Away with you, Satan, for it is written, 'Worship the Lord your God, / and serve only him'" (Matt 4:10). Again, Jesus quotes Moses's instructions to the Israelites, reminding them to worship only the God who brought them out of Egypt. Moses says:

> Take care that you do not forget the LORD, who brought you out of the land of Egypt, out of the house of slavery. The LORD your God you shall fear; him you shall serve, and by his name alone you shall swear. Do not follow other gods, any of the gods of the peoples who are all around you. (Deut 6:12–14)

Jesus, after his forty days in the desert, is about to begin his public ministry. He is going to obey the instructions Moses gave the Israelites after their forty years in the desert as they prepared to enter the promised land; Jesus will live in fidelity to every word that God speaks, he will do what is right and good in the sight of God, and he will not serve political or religious leaders who are in service to themselves. Jesus will do God's will. Having failed to tempt Jesus to prove that he is God's own son by abusing his power, the devil leaves, defeated.

MINISTRY IN GALILEE

Jesus begins his public ministry in Galilee, not in Jerusalem, the religious center and the location of the Temple. Why? Matthew gives us two reasons. Matthew tells us that Jesus moved to Galilee after hearing that John had been arrested. Perhaps Jesus thought it safer to be in Galilee. The second reason is that Jesus was following God's will. Matthew explains this by once more claiming that the words of the prophet were being fulfilled:

> Land of Zebulun and Naphtali
> on the road by the sea, across the Jordan, Galilee of the Gentiles—
> the people who sat in darkness
> have seen a great light
> and for those who sat in the region and shadow of death
> light has dawned. (Matt 4:15–16)

The original setting for this passage from Isaiah 9:1–2 is the Northern Kingdom after it was captured by the Assyrians in 734 BCE. Zebulun and Naphtali are the names of two of the twelve tribes of Israel, two of the ten tribes that made up the Northern Kingdom. Isaiah was offering the people hope that they would one day be liberated from Assyrian rule. By claiming that this passage was fulfilled in Jesus, Matthew teaches that the promised liberation has come. Jesus is the light of the world. Matthew tells us, "From that time Jesus began to proclaim, 'Repent, for the kingdom of heaven has come near'" (Matt 4:17). A new life will dawn for the people if they repent and become disciples of Jesus Christ.

Jesus's public ministry has begun. He calls the first disciples: Peter, Andrew, James, and John. He teaches in synagogues and cures many people so that his reputation spreads far and wide. Great crowds begin to follow Jesus.

THE SERMON ON THE MOUNT

Matthew's account of Jesus giving what is popularly known as "the Sermon on the Mount" is replete with Old Testament allusions. Through this sermon, Matthew pictures Jesus teaching his disciples and the crowd how to live a life of happiness and holiness, how to live so as to please God. At the same time, Matthew once more assures his Jewish audience that Jesus is not rejecting the Law and the prophets, precious to the Jews, but is fulfilling them. To become a disciple of Jesus Christ is not to reject Judaism but to see the covenant with God fulfilled.

First, let us notice the setting. Matthew tells us, "When Jesus saw the crowds, he went up the mountain; and after he sat down, his disciples came to him. Then he began to speak, and taught them" (Matt 5:1–2). Jesus's long sermon (Matt 5:1—7:27) then begins with the Beatitudes.

The Gospel according to Luke also pictures Jesus teaching the Beatitudes, although only four compared to Matthew's nine (see Luke 6:20–22). As Luke introduces Jesus's teaching, Luke says, "He came down with them and stood on a level place, with a great crowd of his disciples and a great multitude of people" (Luke 6:17). So, in Matthew we read the "sermon on the mount," and in Luke we read the "sermon on the plain" (Luke 6:20–49). Is this difference significant? It is. Matthew places Jesus on a mountain to remind his readers of Moses on a mountain, Mount Sinai (also called Mount Horeb), when God gave Moses the Ten Commandments (Exod 19—20). Matthew is telling his audience that Jesus is the new Moses who has God's authority to promulgate a new law, a law that is not a rejection but a fulfillment of the old law.

Remember now what we have said about the literary form of the Gospels. They are edited accounts of oral and written tradition about events. Their core message is accurate, but they do not claim historical accuracy in exact social settings. As editors, both Matthew and Luke chose the physical setting for Jesus's teaching of the Beatitudes. Matthew places Jesus on a mountain because he wants to tie Jesus to Moses and to Jewish covenant history. Luke is writing to Gentiles; he has no reason to do the same.

BEATITUDES

The literary form *beatitude* was common in the Old Testament, particularly in the psalms (for example, see Pss 1:1; 32:1–2; 41:1; 65:4; 84:4–5). A beatitude could begin with the word *happy* or *blessed*. Either way, a beatitude teaches what behavior leads to a person's being free of suffering, happy, and blessed. Righteous behavior puts people in right relationship with God and has its rewards.

Much of the content of Jesus's Beatitudes in Matthew is also found in the Old Testament. For instance, two of the Beatitudes are: "Blessed are those who are persecuted for righteousness' sake, for theirs is the kingdom of heaven" (Matt 5:10), and "Blessed are those who mourn, for they will be comforted" (Matt 5:4). Isaiah, too, offers hope that those who are persecuted and who mourn will be comforted:

> The spirit of the Lord GOD is upon me,
> because the LORD has anointed me;
> he has sent me to bring good news to the oppressed,
> to bind up the broken hearted,
> to proclaim liberty to the captives,
> and release to the prisoners…
> to comfort those who mourn. (Isa 61:1, 2b)

Two more of the Beatitudes are: "Blessed are the meek, for they will inherit the earth" (Matt 5:5), and "Blessed are the pure in heart, for they will see God" (Matt 5:8). The psalms also teach that the meek and the pure of heart will be blessed. For instance, in Psalm 37 we read:

> But the meek will inherit the land,
> and delight themselves in abundant prosperity. (Ps 37:11)

In Psalm 24 we read:

> Those who have clean hands and pure hearts,
> who do not lift up their souls to what is false,
> and do not swear deceitfully.
> They will receive blessing from the LORD. (Ps 24:4–5a)

However, Jesus expands rather than simply repeats the lessons of the psalms. This is because the Israelites did not come to a belief in life after death until after the Babylonian exile. The Beatitudes in the psalms teach that right behavior is rewarded on earth.

For instance, Psalm 41 begins:

Happy are those who consider the poor;
  the LORD delivers them in the day of trouble.
The LORD protects them and keeps them alive;
  they are called happy in the land.
  You do not give them up to the will of their enemies.
The LORD sustains them on their sickbed;
  in their illness you heal all their infirmities. (Ps 41:1–3)

Jesus teaches that right behavior is rewarded not just in this life but in the "kingdom of heaven." In Matthew, Jesus's first Beatitude is, "Blessed are the poor in spirit, for theirs is the kingdom of heaven" (Matt 5:3). This first Beatitude sets the context for all the Beatitudes that follow. Jesus's last Beatitude is, "Blessed are you when people revile you and persecute you and utter all kinds of evil against you falsely on my account. Rejoice and be glad, for your reward is great in heaven" (Matt 5:11–12).

We will discuss further the meaning of the *kingdom of heaven*, called the *kingdom of God* in parallel passages in the Gospel according to Mark, one of Matthew's sources, in a later chapter.

TO FULFILL, NOT ABOLISH, THE LAW AND THE PROPHETS

As Jesus continues his Sermon on the Mount, he specifically states that his expanded teaching is not a rejection of the Law and the prophets but a fulfillment of them. Jesus stands on the shoulders of his ancestors. He says, "Do not think that I have come to abolish the law or the prophets; I have come not to abolish but to fulfill" (Matt 5:17). He then introduces his teaching with the repeated phrase, "You have heard that it was said...But I say to you..." (Matt 5:21–22, 27–28, 33–34, 43–44).

In Jesus's first expansion of the Law he says, "You have heard that it was said to those of ancient times, 'You shall not murder'; and 'whoever murders shall be liable to judgment.' But I say to you that if you are angry with a brother or sister, you will be liable to judgment" (Matt 5:21–22a). He goes on to say that if you insult another person, you will be held accountable.

"You shall not murder" is one of the Ten Commandments and appears in both Exodus and Deuteronomy (see Exod 20:13; Deut 5:17). The time of the setting in both accounts is the time of the Israelites' exodus from Egypt (1250 BCE) and their forty years in the desert, when Moses received the Ten Commandments and taught them to the people. The Ten Commandments are the social expression of God's covenant relationship with God's people.

However, the Book of Exodus, in its present form, was written with hindsight. While based on oral and written traditions about events, the material was edited several times, the final time being after the Babylonian exile (587 BCE) when the exiles had returned to Judah.

The Book of Deuteronomy, too, was written long after the events described. As we said earlier, Deuteronomy was also edited after the Babylonian exile had ended. Lessons learned from the fall of the Northern Kingdom to the Assyrians (721 BCE) and the exile are included in the narrative. Just as the Israelites were entering the promised land after leaving Egypt, so were the returning exiles entering Judah after their exile in Babylon. The returning exiles are being taught what Moses's contemporaries were being taught: how to live in loving fidelity to the covenant that God has made with them.

Jesus expands the injunction not to murder by addressing not just exterior actions—killing someone—but also interior motivations. Are you angry? Anger, which leads one to insult others and to treat others disrespectfully, will also be judged.

This pattern continues. "You shall not commit adultery" is also one of the Ten Commandments (see Exod 20:14; Deut 5:18). Again, not just the exterior action but the interior disposition that leads to the action—lust—is condemned. Divorce is allowed in Deuteronomy (see Deut 24:1). Once more Jesus is more demanding than the Law. A man who divorces his wife for trivial reasons, gives her a certificate of divorce, and then marries another is also committing adultery.

The prohibition against swearing falsely is taught in the Book of Leviticus (19:12), in Numbers (30:2), and in Deuteronomy (23:21). The Book of Leviticus was written after the Babylonian exile when the Israelites were back in their land but not under self-rule. In the absence of kings and prophets, priests had the primary leadership role in the lives of the returned exiles. Leviticus contains many ritual instructions for priests, who were of the tribe of Levi. That is why the book is named Leviticus. The Book of Leviticus instructs the people how to be holy, to live in fidelity to covenant love. Once more, the setting for the book is Mount Sinai and the time of Moses (1250 BCE). However, the law promulgated by the book developed over the centuries between the exodus and the end of the Babylonian exile.

Chapter 19 of Leviticus begins: "The LORD spoke to Moses, saying: 'Speak to all the congregation of the people of Israel and say to them: You shall be holy, for I the LORD your God am holy'" (19:1–2). The people are to be holy because God, who is holy, has chosen them to be God's own people, and God dwells in their midst. One way in which the people are to be holy is not to swear in God's name and then not keep their oath: "And you shall not swear falsely by my name, profaning the name of your God: I am the LORD" (Lev 19:12).

The Book of Numbers has the same setting as does Leviticus: the time of Moses. In Numbers, the people are preparing to leave Mount Sinai and travel to the promised land. While at Sinai, censuses were taken of the people. The Book of Numbers is named after those censuses. Once again, the final editors of the book are priests who were leading and instructing the returned exiles after the Babylonian exile. In Numbers, Moses is pictured as teaching, "When a man makes a vow to the LORD, or swears an oath to bind himself by a pledge, he shall not break his word; he shall do according to all that proceeds out of his mouth" (Num 30:1–2).

Jesus builds on this law by teaching that people should not swear at all. Swearing implies that you must tell the truth if you are under oath, but you need not tell the truth if you are not under oath. Jesus says, "Let you word be 'Yes, Yes' or 'No, No'; anything more than this comes from the evil one" (Matt 5:37). In other words, tell the truth all the time.

Jesus then goes on to teach against retaliation, saying, "You have heard that it was said, 'An eye for an eye and a tooth for a tooth'" (Matt 5:38). Permission to punish your enemy to the same degree to which your enemy has harmed you appears in Exodus (21:23–24), in Leviticus (24:19–20), and in Deuteronomy (19:21). For instance, Leviticus says, "Anyone who maims another shall suffer the same injury in return: fracture for fracture, eye for eye, tooth for tooth; the injury inflicted is the injury to be suffered" (24:19–20).

Jesus's injunction regarding retribution is a perfect example of how Jesus does not deny the truth taught in the Law but builds on that truth, enjoining his followers to act radically in the direction of love. The teaching against revenge was a step forward in understanding what it means to love one's neighbor. The injunction against revenge is challenging. As an example: If someone harmed one of my children, I can imagine being so angry that I would want to annihilate that person. What right does he/she have even to exist? The Law taught a step in the right direction, toward love, when it required that I not do worse to the person who harmed my child than the harm that person did to the child. Jesus teaches even more radically in the direction of love. A person's harming my child does not give me the right to harm that person. I must forgive and treat that person with love. If I did that, I would be giving the person a witness of God's love. Maybe such an experience would change that person's whole life. Disciples of Jesus Christ are taught not to retaliate, but to "turn the other cheek" (Matt 5:39).

Jesus then further expands how we are to love others. He says, "You have heard that it was said, 'You shall love your neighbor and hate your enemy.' But I say to you, Love your enemies and pray for those who persecute you" (Matt 5:43–44). Here Jesus is referring to the Book of Leviticus, which says, "You shall not hate in your heart anyone of your kin; you shall reprove your neighbor, or you will incur guilt yourself. You shall not take vengeance or bear a grudge against any of your people, but you shall love your neighbor as yourself: I am the LORD" (19:17–18).

The Israelites understood that they should love their fellow Israelites, but they did not understand that they should love the people of other nations, especially those who had persecuted them. Jesus proclaims that all of God's children, not just those of our own religion or our own country, are our neighbors. Luke pictures Jesus teaching this same truth to a Jewish lawyer, that he is to love even Samaritans, whom the lawyer considered unclean (see Luke 10:25–37). We read about this teaching coming to fruition in chapter 10 of the Acts of the Apostles when Peter has a vision and realizes that he is to go to the home of Cornelius, a Gentile. This teaching would be very important to Matthew's Jewish audience who were having to accept Gentiles, who did not obey the Jewish law, as fellow disciples of Jesus Christ.

Jesus's *fulfilling* or *expanding* the law in regard to "an eye for an eye" and in regard to whom we are required to love gives us the opportunity to identify a third context to consider when discerning what the inspired word of God is saying to us. We have already considered the first two contexts: literary form and the presumed knowledge shared by the author and his contemporary audience. A third context is the place of a teaching in the overarching narrative that is presented in the collection of books that we call the Bible.

People who fail to consider this context sometimes claim that the Bible contradicts itself. They see "an eye for an eye" as contradicting "Love your enemy." When we put these teachings in their historical contexts and consider the overarching narrative, we see that they are not contradictory. They are steps in a process of revelation, each demanding a more loving response than the previous teaching.

Jesus reveals that God is love. Disciples of Jesus Christ are called to be witnesses of that love to all we meet—no exceptions.

One more important point to notice is the recurring phrase Jesus uses as he expands the law: "You have heard that it was said...but I say...." To understand the significance of these words we must recall the literary form, oracle, which is common to the prophets. Prophets would begin their teaching by saying, "Thus says the Lord." Prophets spoke for God. That is what the word *prophet* means—one who speaks for another.

Given that tradition, for Jesus to quote the Law that God gave to Moses and then say, "but I say..." rather than saying, "Thus says the Lord" is astounding. Who is this Jesus that he speaks with such authority? The true answer to this question dawns slowly on the apostles. They do not fully understand the truth until after the resurrection. Jesus is God's own son. Matthew reveals this profound truth in his genealogy and in his birth narrative, and he continues to do so throughout Jesus's Sermon on the Mount.

As Jesus continues his Sermon on the Mount, he instructs against any kind of ostentation when giving alms, praying, and fasting. As part of his instructions on how to pray, Jesus teaches the Our Father:

> Our Father in heaven,
> hallowed be your name.
> Your kingdom come,
> Your will be done,
> on earth as it is in heaven.
> Give us this day our daily bread.
> And forgive us our debts,
> as we also have forgiven our debtors.
> And do not bring us to the time of trial,
> but rescue us from the evil one. (Matt 6:9–13)

In this prayer Jesus begins to reveal that God's kingdom is already established in heaven and is in the process of being established on earth. "Your kingdom come, / Your will be done, / on earth as it is in heaven" is an example of parallel structure, a device often used in Hebrew poetry. In parallel structure, the author expresses the same idea in different words in two adjacent lines. "Your kingdom come" and "Your will be done" are saying the same thing. God's kingdom exists wherever God's will is being done, "on earth as it is in heaven."

Jesus is preaching the kingdom, but not the kingdom of David. Jesus is teaching about a kingdom in which God's will reigns, a kingdom that unites heaven and earth.

After warning his listeners to serve God, not wealth, to trust God's providential care, and to refrain from judging others, Jesus reminds them of the golden rule: "In everything do to others as you would have them do to you: for this is the law and the prophets" (Matt 7:12). With this teaching, Jesus once more expresses his deep respect for, and allegiance to, his inherited traditions. He has not come to abolish the Law and the prophets but to fulfill them.

As Jesus concludes his lengthy sermon, Matthew comments, "Now when Jesus had finished saying these things, the crowds were astounded at his teaching, for he taught them as one having authority, and not as their scribes" (Matt 7:28–29). Jesus taught as one having God's own authority. Matthew will continue to emphasize Jesus's unique authority throughout his Gospel.

5

JESUS'S AUTHORITY AND THE APOSTOLIC MISSION

To understand the second of the five sections in Matthew's Gospel that appear between the birth narratives and the passion narrative, each consisting of stories about Jesus and a sermon by Jesus, we again need to understand the allusions the author makes to the Old Testament. While this second section (Matt 8:1—10:42) does not directly teach the relationship between Jesus's teachings and the law that Moses received from God, as did the first section, it nevertheless relies on the ability of Matthew's Jewish audience to understand many Old Testament allusions.

This section of Matthew's account begins with Jesus curing a leper. If you were a Jew in the audience contemporary with Matthew, this story would puzzle you. Is Jesus a faithful Jew, observing Jewish purity laws, or not?

The story begins with a leper coming to Jesus, kneeling before him, and saying, "Lord, if you choose, you can make me clean" (Matt 8:2). According to purity laws, this is not the way a leper is supposed to behave. The law in Leviticus teaches that "the person who has the leprous disease shall wear torn clothes and let the hair of his head be disheveled; and he shall cover his upper lip and cry out, 'Unclean, unclean.' He shall remain unclean as long as he has the disease; he is unclean. He shall live alone; his dwelling shall be outside the camp" (Lev 13:45–46). What is this leper doing, joining a crowd and approaching Jesus?

Jesus does not reject the leper; Jesus "stretched out his hand and touched him, saying, 'I do choose. Be made clean!'" (Matt 8:3). Jesus did not admonish the leper for approaching him. Rather, Jesus touched him! Does Jesus care nothing about the law when it comes to how a leper should isolate himself? Jesus shows that he does know the law and respects it; he instructs the now cleansed leper to "show yourself to the priest, and offer the gift that Moses commanded, as a testimony to them" (Matt 8:4). Chapters 13 and 14 of the Book of Leviticus detail how a person with leprosy is to present himself to a priest and have himself be declared clean or unclean. Prescribed rituals must take place before the leper is declared clean and is readmitted to society. Jesus directs the now cured leper to obey this law.

By the time of Jesus's public ministry, the Jews had developed many purity laws that declared whether they were clean or unclean. Some of these laws involved totally exterior behavior, such as declaring some foods clean and other foods unclean, some people clean and others unclean (Samaritans, Gentiles). Some of the laws involved moral behavior. Jesus seems to be observant of laws that regarded moral behavior: Are you loving your neighbor and acting for your neighbor's good, or are you excluding your neighbor? Jesus did not always observe laws that involved only exterior behavior. Those laws sometimes resulted in a person's feeling justified in excluding others and therefore failing to act lovingly toward some of God's beloved children.

We see Jesus's constantly inclusive behavior in Matthew's next miracle story in which Jesus heals a centurion's servant. A centurion was a Roman soldier who had authority over one hundred men. He was a Gentile. When the centurion asks that Jesus heal his servant, Jesus immediately offers to go to the centurion's home. To enter the home of a Gentile, an uncircumcised man who eats unclean food, would, in the eyes of some of Jesus's Jewish contemporaries, have made Jesus unclean (see Acts 11:1–3). The centurion evidently is aware of the purity laws for he says, "Lord, I am not worthy to have you come under my roof; but only speak the word, and my servant will be healed" (Matt 8:8).

Jesus compares the centurion's faith to the lack of faith in some of his Jewish critics. He says, "Truly I tell you, many will come from east and west and will eat with Abraham and Isaac and Jacob in the kingdom of heaven, while the heirs of the kingdom will be thrown into the outer darkness, where there will be weeping and gnashing of teeth" (Matt 8:10b–12). Jesus is not rejecting his Jewish heritage. He is simply teaching that God's covenant with Abraham will include more than the Israelites. Many will come from the east and west and become one with God's chosen people.

Matthew then tells us that Jesus continued his healing ministry by curing Peter's mother-in-law, casting out demons from those possessed, and curing the sick. Matthew adds, "This was to fulfill what had been spoken through the prophet Isaiah, 'He took our infirmities and bore our diseases'" (Matt 8:17). This quotation is from Isaiah 53:4, from one of Isaiah's suffering servant songs.

ISAIAH'S SUFFERING SERVANT SONGS

The Book of Isaiah is thought to include the work of three prophets in three different time periods: before the Babylonian exile (chapters 1—39), during the Babylonian exile (chapters 40—55), and after the Babylonian exile (chapters 56—66). For this reason, chapters 40—55 are referred to as Second Isaiah.

The prophecies in Second Isaiah are offering hope to the exiles in Babylon that God still loves them and that their suffering is not in vain. Rather, God is accomplishing something wonderful through them. Their suffering will soon come to an end, and all nations will come to recognize Israel's God. In teaching this good news, and in probing the mystery of innocent suffering, Second Isaiah includes four Suffering Servant songs (Isa 42:1–7; 49:1–7; 50:4–9; 52:13—53:12). It is Isaiah's fourth Suffering Servant song that Matthew is quoting when, after describing Jesus's many acts of healing power, Matthew says, "This was to fulfill what had been spoken through the prophet Isaiah, 'He took our infirmities and bore our diseases'" (Matt 8:17). In quoting this passage, Matthew is applying a Suffering Servant song to Jesus.

We know from the Acts of the Apostles that the early Church used the Suffering Servant songs to probe the mystery of innocent suffering and to try to understand what had been accomplished through Jesus's suffering, death, and resurrection (see Acts 8:26–40). In Acts, Philip encounters an Ethiopian who was reading the prophet Isaiah. The passage he was reading was from the fourth Suffering Servant song:

> Like a sheep he was led to the slaughter,
> and like a lamb silent before its shearer,
> so he does not open his mouth.
>
> In his humiliation justice was denied him.
> Who can describe his generation?
> For his life is taken away from the earth. (Acts 8:32b–33)

The Ethiopian asks Philip whether the prophet was referring to himself or to someone else. "Then Philip began to speak, and starting with this scripture, he proclaimed to him the good news about Jesus" (Acts 8:35).

In the context of Second Isaiah, the Suffering Servant, who remained faithful to God even while innocently suffering, was the nation, Israel, in exile in Babylon. In the context of the Gospel according to Matthew, the Suffering Servant is reinterpreted to be Jesus Christ. Matthew uses the passage from the Suffering Servant song—"He took our infirmities and bore our diseases"—to explain what was being accomplished through Jesus and his healings. In the light of the resurrection, Matthew is teaching his Jewish contemporaries that what Isaiah's Suffering Servant was to accomplish for all nations has been accomplished through Jesus Christ.

As great crowds follow Jesus, a scribe approaches Jesus and offers to follow him. Jesus replies, "Foxes have holes, and birds of the air have nests; but the Son of Man has nowhere to lay his head" (Matt 8:20). In this reply, Jesus is pictured not only warning the scribe about the difficulties of discipleship and the wholehearted commitment necessary to become a true disciple of Jesus but also revealing something about his own identity and role by referring to himself as the "Son of Man."

THE SON OF MAN

"Son of Man" is a messianic title that would have been familiar to a Jewish scribe because a scribe's role was to preserve and teach his fellow Jews the Scriptures. "Son of Man" is the only messianic title that Jesus uses in relationship to himself. The title is an allusion to the Book of Daniel.

The Book of Daniel was written in the second century BCE during a time of persecution under Antiochus Epiphanes (175–164 BCE). While the author lived in the second century BCE, he set his book in the sixth century BCE, before and during the Babylonian exile. The author uses two different literary forms: stories told to teach moral lessons and a form popular for a four-hundred-year span (200 BCE–200 CE) called *apocalyptic literature*. *Apocalyptic literature* was written to persecuted people, offering them hope that their suffering would soon be over. It was written in code so that the persecuted audience would understand it, but the persecutors would not. There are two examples of apocalyptic books in the Christian Bible: the Book of Daniel in the Old Testament and the Book of Revelation in the New Testament.

In chapter 7 of the Book of Daniel, Daniel has a vision of the heavenly court with God sitting on God's throne. Daniel says:

> I gazed into the visions of the night.
> And I saw, coming on the clouds of heaven,
> one like a son of man.
> He came to the one of great age
> and was led into his presence.
> On him was conferred sovereignty,
> glory, and kingship,
> and men of all peoples, nations and languages became his servants.
> His sovereignty is an eternal sovereignty
> which shall never pass away,
> nor will his empire ever be destroyed. (Dan 7:13–14; Jerusalem Bible translation)

As we continue to read the Gospel according to Matthew, we will see that the messianic title "Son of Man" will be used twenty-eight times. By referring to himself as Son of Man, Jesus is pictured as revealing that he is, indeed, the longed-for messiah. However, as we see the title used in later passages, Jesus will be teaching his followers that this messianic figure will be different from the messiah whom they were anticipating. This Son of Man will undergo great suffering, be killed, and will be raised on the third day (see Matt 16:13–23).

WHAT SORT OF MAN IS THIS?

Matthew next tells us the story of Jesus calming a storm. The disciples are on a boat with Jesus when a storm arises. The disciples are terrified. They wake Jesus up and plead, "Lord, save us! We are perishing" (Matt 8:25). Jesus wakes up and asks, "Why are you afraid, you of little faith?" (Matt 8:26). Jesus then calms the storm. The disciples ask one another, "What sort of man is this, that even the winds and the sea obey him?" (Matt 8:27).

This story is a perfect example of the literary form *miracle story.* A *miracle story* presents a problem, shows Jesus being made aware of the problem, describes Jesus solving the problem, and describes those present showing amazement at what they have witnessed. The observers' amazement centers the reader's attention on the identity of Jesus.

A person familiar with Jewish Scriptures would recognize that this story of Jesus calming a storm brings to mind Psalm 107, a psalm of thanksgiving. In Psalm 107 we read:

> Some went down to the sea in ships,
> doing business on the mighty waters;
> they saw the deeds of the LORD,
> his wondrous works in the deep.
> For he commanded and raised the stormy wind,
> which lifted up the waves of the sea.
> They mounted up to heaven, they went down to the depths;
> their courage melted away in their calamity;

they reeled and staggered like drunkards,
and were at their wits' end.
Then they cried to the Lord in their trouble,
and he brought them out from their distress;
he made the storm be still,
and the waves of the sea were hushed.
Then they were glad because they had quiet,
and he brought them to their desired haven.
Let them thank the Lord for his steadfast love,
for his wonderful works to humankind. (Ps 107:23–31)

"What sort of man is this, that even the winds and the sea obey him?" Through his allusion to Psalm 107, Matthew teaches that Jesus is the Messiah, the son of God. Who else could calm a ferocious storm?

THE DEMONS ENTER THE SWINE?

Matthew's next story recounts Jesus expelling demons from two possessed men, allowing the demons to enter some swine, and the swine suddenly rushing down the hill into the sea and drowning (Matt 8:28–34). This is one of the strangest stories in the Gospels. However, knowledge of literary form makes the story much more understandable. Everything we have just explained about the form of the *miracle story* and *apocalyptic literature* will help us correctly understand the story. As we will see, this story, too, depends on knowledge of the Old Testament in order to discern all of its meaning.

First, let us note that the story on a surface level is puzzling. Why did the demons want to enter the pigs? Why did Jesus let them? Didn't Jesus care that the pigs belonged to the swineherds, and they needed them as a source of their livelihood?

In terms of literary form, the story does not match the form of a miracle story, as did the story of Jesus's calming the storm. Notice the ending: rather than having those who witness Jesus's mighty actions being in awe and, by their reaction, centering our attention on Jesus's identity, the observers are upset, and they tell their townspeople what has happened, who then ask Jesus to leave.

In probing the meaning of this story, Scripture scholars encourage us to compare Matthew's account to a similar story in the Gospel according to Mark (see Mark 5:1–20). Remember, Mark's Gospel is one of the written sources used by the author of Matthew's Gospel. Following this advice, we will first look at the story as it appears in Mark, clarifying its literary form and its message. We will then ask: Why did Matthew make the changes he did? What is the point that Matthew wants to make through his version of the story? Are there Old Testament allusions in this text?

The story in Mark takes place in a different location, in Gerasa, not in Gadara. In Mark only one person is possessed, not two. Mark's story describes a conversation between the demon and Jesus in which Jesus asks the demon, "'What is your name?' The demon replied, 'My name is Legion; for we are many'" (Mark 5:9). Matthew omits this interchange. In Mark, the demons ask permission to enter the herd of swine that is grazing nearby. Jesus gives the demons "permission" to enter the swine. Mark tells us that once the demons entered the swine, "the herd, numbering about two thousand, rushed down the steep bank into the sea, and were drowned in the sea" (Mark 5:13). Matthew does not tell us the number of swine. Why all the changes?

Matthew and Mark write for different audiences with different needs. Mark is writing in about 65 CE to an audience suffering persecution in Rome. Their lives are in danger. This story is an example of apocalyptic writing. It is a story, written in code to a persecuted audience, offering them hope that their persecution will soon end. Good will triumph over evil. God will save them.

Mark gives those in his audience a heads-up that they should look for a hidden meaning by including some plot elements that the audience would recognize as signals. Mark's setting is the land of the Gerasenes. Gerasa is not by the sea. Nevertheless, the plot has the swine drowning in the sea. Then Mark's account stresses military terminology: The demons say their name is *Legion*. The word *legion* refers to a division of Roman soldiers that included thousands of troops. A "herd of pigs" was a derogatory way of referring to a group of military recruits. Mark's military language continues: the demons are given *permission to enter* the pigs. Mark tells us that two thousand pigs are drowned, a reference to "Legion." So, through code, Mark is offering persecuted Christians hope that, just as God saved their ancestors at the time of the exodus and the parting of the sea, thus allowing them to escape the Egyptian army (who drowned pursuing the Israelites), so will God save them from their Roman persecutors (the "pigs" who drowned). They should persevere in faith and hope because the end time, the end of their present persecution, is near.

Matthew's audience is not suffering persecution and is not living in Rome. Matthew writes about 80 CE to Jewish Christians living in Antioch, Syria. His main message is that Jesus is the fulfillment of God's promises to God's chosen people through the centuries. To have faith in Jesus is to remain faithful to covenant love. Matthew retains the parts of the story that support his theme: Jesus is the Son of God, and Jesus has authority over evil spirits. He also retains the allusion to the exodus, to the drowning of the pursuing army.

However, Matthew changes the parts of the story that were signals to Mark's audience to look for a hidden message about the final defeat of their Roman persecutors. By changing the location to Gadara, Matthew places the action closer to the sea. The land of the Gadarenes (see Matt 8:28) is six miles from the sea, while Gerasa (see Mark 5:1) is thirty miles from the sea. By not including the demon's name, Legion, the formal permission given by Jesus to the demons, and the number of pigs, two thousand, Matthew omits the military language and references to Roman soldiers.

Matthew's story centers his audience's attention on the identity of Jesus as the Son of God and on Jesus's authority. Even the demons recognize Jesus. They say, "What have you to do with us, Son of God?" (Matt 8:29). They also recognize Jesus's authority, begging him, "If you cast us out, send us into the herd of swine" (Matt 8:31). As we continue to read Matthew's Gospel, the emphasis will remain on Jesus's identity and authority.

For instance, in Matthew's story of Jesus healing a paralytic, Jesus once more refers to himself as the "Son of Man," the messianic title from the Book of Daniel. Some men bring a paralytic to Jesus. Instead of physically healing the man, Jesus forgives him his sins. Scribes who were present thought that Jesus was blaspheming. Only God can forgive sins. Jesus then demonstrates that there is authority behind his words.

He challenges the scribes, saying, "'But so that you may know that the Son of Man has authority on earth to forgive sins'—he then said to the paralytic—'Stand up, take your bed and go to your home.' And he stood up and went to his home" (Matt 9:6–7).

Jesus is challenged again, this time by the Pharisees. After calling Matthew to follow him, Jesus is having dinner with tax collectors and sinners. The Pharisees ask why Jesus keeps such unsavory company. In answering, Jesus quotes the Book of Hosea (Hos 6:6), saying, "Go and learn what this means, 'I desire mercy, not sacrifice,' for I have come to call not the righteous but sinners" (Matt 9:13).

The prophet Hosea lived in the Northern Kingdom before it was conquered by the Assyrians in 721 BCE. Hosea had an unfaithful wife whom he continued to love and whom he wished would return to him. He saw his own situation as a metaphor for the relationship between the Northern Kingdom and God. The people were being unfaithful to covenant love, worshipping other gods, but God, who still loved them, longed for their return and their faithfulness. Hosea pictures God saying to God's people, "For I desire steadfast love and not sacrifice, the knowledge of God rather than burnt offerings" (Hos 6:6).

When Jesus tells the Pharisees that he has come "to call not the righteous but sinners," Jesus is speaking ironically. Jesus has come to call everyone. Jesus is calling the Pharisees, too. The problem is that those Pharisees who disapprove of Jesus do not realize that, because of their judgmental and self-righteous behavior, they, too, are sinners.

Jesus is next challenged by the disciples of John the Baptist. They ask, "Why do we and the Pharisees fast often, but your disciples do not fast?" (Matt 9:14). Jesus's answer is once again centered on his identity. However, to understand his answer, one must know something about what the Old Testament teaches about fasting.

There are numerous examples of people fasting in the Old Testament. Some fasting was by individuals and some fasting was as a whole community. An individual might fast as an expression of mourning, of contrition, or to seek God's assistance. In Jesus's time, some Pharisees fasted twice a week (see Luke 18:12). Old Testament prophets also warned against letting fasting become a meaningless ritual. For instance, the prophet Isaiah warns against fasting becoming a show to draw attention to oneself and one's "virtue" rather than resulting in loving service to others. Isaiah pictures God saying:

> Look, you serve your own interest on your fast day,
> and oppress all your workers.
> Look, you fast only to quarrel and to fight
> and to strike with a wicked fist.
> Such fasting as you do today
> will not make your voice heard on high....
> Is not this the fast that I choose;
> to loose the bonds of injustice,
> to undo the thongs of the yoke,
> to let the oppressed go free,
> and to break every yoke? (Isa 58:3b–4, 6)

Jesus is not objecting to fasting. He himself fasted for forty days in the desert. Rather, he uses the occasion to reveal something about his own identity. Jesus says, "The wedding guests cannot mourn as long as the bridegroom is with them, can they? The days will come when the bridegroom is taken away from them, and then they will fast" (Matt 9:15).

Here, Jesus compares himself to the bridegroom. As we just mentioned, in the Book of Hosea, God is compared to a faithful husband with an unfaithful wife:

> On that day, says the Lord, you will call me, "My husband," and no longer will you call me, "My Baal." For I will remove the names of the Baals from her mouth, and they shall be mentioned by name no more. I will make for you a covenant on that day with the wild animals, the birds of the air, and the creeping things of the ground; and I will abolish the bow, the sword, and war from the land; and I will make you lie down in safety. And I will take you for my wife forever; I will take you for my wife in righteousness and in justice, in steadfast love, and in mercy. I will take you for my wife in faithfulness, and you shall know the Lord. (Hos 2:16–20)

By comparing himself to the bridegroom, Jesus is implying his divinity. Why? Because fasting is a way to seek God's power and intervention. Through Jesus, who is the Son of God, God is already present, just as the bridegroom is present. There is no reason to fast now. Rather, it is a time to celebrate God's presence in Jesus. Once Jesus is taken away, Jesus's followers will fast once more.

THE NECESSITY OF FAITH

As the stories of Jesus having authority to heal people from a wide variety of human ailments continue, Matthew emphasizes not only Jesus's identity but also the necessity of faith. As faith is emphasized, allusions to the Old Testament continue.

First, a synagogue leader tells Jesus that, even though his daughter has died, Jesus could bring her back to life. This father has great faith. Next, a woman who would be considered unclean approaches Jesus. This woman, who has suffered from hemorrhages for twelve years, should never have been in a crowd and touching Jesus's cloak. She should have kept her distance. Jesus does not correct her for breaking the law but affirms her for her faith. Then blind men who seek Jesus's help call Jesus "Son of David." Matthew has been emphasizing that Jesus is the Son of David from the first sentence of his Gospel as he begins his genealogy. Jesus specifically asks the blind men, "Do you believe that I am able to do this?" (Matt 9:28). They affirm their faith in Jesus's power and call him "Lord" (Matt 9:28b). Some Pharisees, who do not believe in Jesus's identity but cannot deny his authority, conclude that the power that resides in Jesus is the power of demons, not the power of God.

As Matthew concludes his account of Jesus's mighty acts, he says, "Then Jesus went about all the cities and villages, teaching in their synagogues, and proclaiming the good news of the kingdom, and curing every disease and every sickness. When he saw the crowds, he had compassion for them, because they were harassed and helpless, like sheep without a shepherd" (Matt 9:35–36).

The image of the people of Israel being sheep without a shepherd is used over and over in the Old Testament. For instance, in the Book of Numbers, when God tells Moses that he will not be leading the people into Canaan (1210 BCE), Moses asks God to "appoint someone over the congregation who shall go out before them and come in before them, who shall lead them out and bring them in, so that the congregation of the LORD may not be like sheep without a shepherd" (Num 27:16–17).

Ezekiel (593–571 BCE) uses the same imagery when he remonstrates with Israel's leaders, saying,

> The word of the LORD came to me: Mortal, prophesy against the shepherds of Israel: prophesy and say to them—to the shepherds: Thus says the Lord GOD: Ah, you shepherds of Israel who have been feeding yourselves! Should not shepherds feed the sheep?...My sheep were scattered, they wandered over all the mountains and on every high hill; my sheep were scattered over all the face of the earth, with no one to search or seek for them....For thus says the Lord GOD: I myself will search for my sheep, and will seek them out. (Ezek 34:1–2, 6, 11)

(For additional uses of this imagery see 2 Chronicles 18:16 and Zechariah 13:7.)

Before Matthew pictures Jesus beginning his missionary discourse, he describes Jesus appointing the twelve apostles. Matthew says: "Then Jesus summoned his twelve disciples and gave them authority over unclean spirits, to cast them out, and to cure every disease and every sickness. These are the names of the twelve apostles" (Matt 10:1–2a). Notice that Matthew first uses the word *disciple* (which means *learner* or *student*) and then uses the word *apostle* (which means *one sent*) to name the Twelve. In each instance, the number is twelve. Why is the number twelve so important? Once again, this is an allusion to the Old Testament, this time to the twelve tribes of Israel. Matthew makes this clear later in his Gospel when Peter asks Jesus what he and the other disciples will have for leaving everything and following Jesus. Jesus responds, "Truly, I tell you, at the renewal of all things, when the Son of Man is seated on the throne of his glory, you who have followed me will also sit on twelve thrones, judging the twelve tribes of Israel" (Matt 19:28).

THE MISSIONARY DISCOURSE

In this second narrative/discourse section of Matthew's Gospel, Jesus's sermon consists of instructions to his disciples. Jesus is teaching the disciples how they are to carry out their mission, and how they will be treated as a result. This sermon (Matt 10:5–42) is much shorter than the Sermon on the Mount. Nevertheless, it includes five allusions to the Old Testament.

Jesus begins his instructions by saying, "Go nowhere among the Gentiles, and enter no town of the Samaritans, but go rather to the lost sheep of the house of Israel" (Matt 10:5–6). We have already discussed the often-used Old Testament image of Israel being lost sheep who need a shepherd who will take care of them, and God claiming that God will shepherd them.

These instructions surprise today's readers because Jesus seems to be limiting the disciples' ministry to the Israelites and excluding Samaritans and Gentiles. The instructions remind us of the third context within which we must read biblical passages, the context of an overall, developing narrative. Jesus is not excluding Gentiles. He is instructing his disciples to go first to the Israelites, God's chosen people. We know Matthew understands Jesus's mission to have later included the Gentiles from the instructions he pictures Jesus giving to the disciples after his resurrection: "Go therefore and make disciples of all nations, baptizing them in the name of the Father and of the Son and of the Holy Spirit, and teaching them to obey everything that I have commanded you" (Matt 28:19–20a).

As Jesus instructs his disciples to take nothing with them on their journey but to rely on the hospitality of those whom they serve, Jesus says, "laborers deserve their food" (Matt 10:10b). This teaching appears in the Book of Numbers. In this book God instructs Moses to tell the Levites how they are to use the tithe that they receive from the Israelites. The word *Levites* refers to the priests and workers who served the Lord in the Israelites' holy places: their tent of meeting, their tabernacle, and later, their Temple. The Israelites supported the Levites through a tithe that they received for their service (see Num 18:31). Jesus is teaching his disciples that they, like the Levites, deserve to receive the necessities of life as an offering from their fellow Israelites.

Jesus also instructs his disciples how to respond to those who refuse to welcome them: "If anyone will not welcome you or listen to your words, shake off the dust from your feet as you leave that house or town. Truly I tell you, it will be more tolerable for the land of Sodom and Gomorrah on the day of judgment than for that town" (Matt 10:14–15).

We read about why Jesus uses the towns of Sodom and Gomorrah as examples of the heavy price paid for extreme sinfulness in the Book of Genesis (see Genesis 19:1–29). Two angels are sent by God to visit Sodom and Gomorrah because God has heard of their sinfulness: "Then the LORD said, 'How great is the outcry against Sodom and Gomorrah and how very grave their sin! I must go down and see whether they have done altogether according to the outcry that has come to me; and if not, I will know'" (Gen 18:20–21). Lot, who is Abraham's nephew, is sitting at the city gate. He welcomes the guests and offers them hospitality. However, later that evening, all the men of Sodom, "both young and old, all the people to the last man" (Gen 19:4) surround Lot's house and insist that he send the angels/men out so that they can gang rape them. Lot's guests personally witness these sins against both loving sexual behavior and hospitality. Lot and his family are saved from the destruction to come, but the cities themselves are destroyed.

A tradition of referring to Sodom and Gomorrah as an illustration of evil actions is evident in the prophetic books. For example, Jeremiah pictures God saying:

> In the prophets of Samaria
>   I saw a disgusting thing:
> they prophesied by Baal
>   and led my people Israel astray.
> But in the prophets of Jerusalem
>   I have seen a more shocking thing:
> they commit adultery and walk in lies;
>   they strengthen the hands of evildoers
>   so that no one turns from wickedness;
> all of them have become like Sodom to me,
>   and its inhabitants like Gomorrah. (Jer 23:13–14;
>   see also Ezek 16:46–58; Isa 1:10)

Matthew's next allusion to the Old Testament is another reference to the messianic title *Son of Man* that we find in the Book of Daniel. So far, we have seen Jesus use this title in reference to himself when he described the hardship of missionary life ("the Son of Man has no place to lay his head"; Matt 8:20) and when he claimed that he, the Son of Man, has authority on earth to forgive sins (Matt 9:6–7). This time Jesus uses the title in relation to a future coming. Jesus says, "When they persecute you in one town, flee to the next; for truly I tell you, you will not have gone through all the towns of Israel before the Son of Man comes" (Matt 10:23).

To what coming is Jesus referring? Scripture scholars debate this point. Jesus appears to refer to a coming in the lifetime of those to whom he is giving instructions. Is Jesus referring to his own return after his resurrection? As we will soon see, Jesus uses the title Son of Man when he warns the disciples of his future passion, death, and resurrection. Jesus says, "See, we are going up to Jerusalem, and the Son of Man will be handed over to the chief priests and scribes, and they will condemn him to death; then they will hand him over to the Gentiles to be mocked and flogged and crucified; and on the third day he will be raised" (Matt 20:18–19). The coming of the Son of Man is both a present event (Jesus's public ministry) and a future event (Jesus's resurrection).

Jesus next encourages his disciples not to live in fear, even though they will face persecution. After all, God takes care of sparrows, and they are more valuable than many sparrows (Matt 10:31). These comforting words are followed by disturbing words. Jesus says, "Do not think that I have come to bring peace to the earth; I have not come to bring peace, but a sword. For I have come to set a man against his father, and a daughter against her mother, and a daughter-in-law against her mother-in-law; and one's foes will be members of one's own household" (Matt 10:34–36).

In expressing this hard truth, Jesus is not saying that it is his intention or his desire to pit family members against each other. Rather, he knows that family divisions will be the effect of his teaching. Jesus is conveying the same tragic truth that Micah, the prophet of justice, taught both the Northern and Southern Kingdoms in the late eighth century BCE. Micah says, "The faithful have disappeared from the land, / and there is no one left who is upright" (Mic 7:2). Judges ask for bribes. The powerful pervert justice. The time for punishment has come. As examples of this tragic truth, Micah continues:

> Put no trust in a friend,
>   have no confidence in a loved one;
> guard the doors of your mouth
>   from her who lies in your embrace;
> for the son treats the father with contempt,
>   the daughter rises up against her mother,
> the daughter-in-law against her mother-in-law;
>   your enemies are members of your own household.
>   (Mic 7:5–6)

Jesus's missionary discourse does not end on this disturbing note. Rather, Jesus concludes his instructions to the disciples by telling them that they will be rewarded for their faithful service to the preaching of the good news of the kingdom, as will those who welcome them. Welcoming the disciples is the same as welcoming Jesus himself and welcoming God, who sent him (see Matt 10:40–42).

6

RECOGNIZING THE MESSIAH AND THE KINGDOM

In Matthew's third narrative/sermon section (see Matt 11:2—13:52), Matthew is teaching his Jewish contemporaries to recognize that Jesus Christ is the fulfillment of their messianic hopes and that the promised kingdom is already in their midst. However, to reach this understanding, Matthew's contemporaries will have to reinterpret their previous understandings of both *messiah* and *kingdom*. In teaching these messages, Matthew is once again alluding to the Old Testament.

As this third section begins, Matthew immediately centers our attention on the identity of Jesus Christ: "When John heard in prison what the Messiah was doing, he sent word by his disciples and said to him, 'Are you the one who is to come, or are we to wait for another?'" (Matt 11:2–3). Notice in this passage that Matthew, the narrative voice in this Gospel, uses the word *Messiah* and then pictures John's disciples using the words "the one who is to come." At the time in history when Jesus was healing and preaching, his fellow Jews were expecting a messiah, but they did not all have the same idea of the kind of messiah that would be.

The word *messiah* means *the anointed one*. In the Israelite culture, kings, prophets, and priests were anointed. *Messiah* is a Hebrew word. The Greek word for *anointed* is *Christ*. (*Christ* is not Jesus's last name. To say "Jesus Christ" is to say that Jesus is the anointed one.) As we have already discussed in our chapter on Matthew's genealogy, many Israelites through the generations expected a messiah, a son of David, who would establish a kingdom on earth, a geopolitical kingdom, where justice and peace would prevail, where the Israelites would live in the promised land under self-rule.

After the fall of both the Northern Kingdom (721 BCE) and the Southern Kingdom (587 BCE) and the end of the Babylonian exile (537 BCE), the Persians who had conquered the Babylonians allowed the Israelites to return to Judah, but not under self-rule. These events caused some Israelites to begin reimagining the concept of the messiah in apocalyptic terms. The one who would save them would come at the end time on the clouds of heaven. We discussed this messianic hope in chapter 5 when explaining the messianic title that Jesus uses in reference to himself, "Son of Man," an allusion to the Book of Daniel. "The one who is to come" would establish the kingdom sometime in the future.

When Matthew insists that Jesus is the "Son of David," as he has since his genealogy, and when he pictures those seeking healings addressing Jesus as "Son of David," he is affirming that Jesus fulfills the messianic hopes of the Israelites' ancestors, hopes based on the covenant promises made to Abraham and David. When Matthew pictures Jesus referring to himself as "the Son of Man," a reference to apocalyptic hopes in the Book of Daniel, and John the Baptist's disciples asking about "the one who is to come," he is saying that Jesus fulfills the hopes of those apocalyptic expectations. Jesus fulfills all of God's promises and all of the people's expectations through history, different as they are.

When Jesus responds to the question put to him by John the Baptist's disciples, he replies, "Go and tell John what you hear and see: the blind receive their sight, the lame walk, the lepers are cleansed, the deaf hear, the dead are raised, and the poor have good news brought to them. And blessed is anyone who takes no offense at me" (Matt 11:4–6). This must have been a frustrating response for John's disciples. Is it a yes or a no?

When John the Baptist describes the one to come after him earlier in Matthew's Gospel, his description seems to be of a fiery judge. John says, "I baptize you with water for repentance, but one who is more powerful than I is coming after me; He will baptize you with the Holy Spirit and fire. His winnowing fork is in his hand, and he will clear his threshing floor and will gather his wheat into the granary, but the chaff he will burn with unquenchable fire" (Matt 3:11–12). Is this person, Jesus, who is eating and drinking with sinners, the Messiah, or not?

Jesus's answer would have reminded John and his disciples of a passage in Isaiah in which Isaiah offers hope by picturing the exiles returning from Babylon to Jerusalem. God has promised to save them, and God will save them. Isaiah says:

> Then the eyes of the blind shall be opened,
>   and the ears of the deaf unstopped;
> then the lame shall leap like a deer,
>   and the tongue of the speechless sing for joy. (Isa 35:5–6)

By his response, Jesus is reminding John's disciples and John that these are the expected signs of God saving God's people. Jesus is fulfilling these signs in a very literal sense. Is Jesus "the one who is to come" or not? He is. There is no need to look for another.

After this conversation with John the Baptist's disciples about Jesus's identity, Jesus begins to teach the crowd about John's identity. Jesus says, "What then did you go out to see? A prophet? Yes, I tell you, and more than a prophet. This is the one about whom it is written, 'See I am sending my messenger ahead of you, who will prepare your way before you'" (Matt 9:10). Here Jesus is quoting the prophet Malachi. We introduced the prophet Malachi and this quotation from Malachi 3:1 in chapter 4 when discussing the connection between John the Baptist and Elijah. Here Jesus makes that connection explicit when he says, "For all the prophets and the law prophesied until John came; and if you are willing to accept it, he is Elijah who is to come. Let anyone with ears listen" (Matt 11:13–15). What is Jesus implying by saying that John the Baptist is Elijah?

Jesus is saying that John the Baptist is fulfilling the function that had been prophesied by Malachi and associated with Elijah: God would send a messenger who would prepare the way for the expected messiah and for the inauguration of God's kingdom. John the Baptist is God's messenger and is doing just that. In saying this, Jesus is claiming that he himself is the expected messiah since John the Baptist is preparing the way for him.

Jesus then criticizes his contemporaries because they reject both John and Jesus. John is too abstemious, and Jesus, "the Son of Man," is not abstemious enough. What do they want? Once more, notice that Jesus refers to himself as the "Son of Man" (Matt 11:19). As we already know, this is a messianic claim and an allusion to the Book of Daniel.

Jesus also severely criticizes cities in which he has worked mighty signs but that have rejected him. Jesus says, "Woe to you, Chorazin! Woe to you, Bethsaida! For if the deeds of power done in you had been done in Tyre and Sidon, they would have repented long ago in sackcloth and ashes" (Matt 11:21).

Jesus's Jewish contemporaries would have known about Tyre and Sidon, two ancient Gentile port cities on the Mediterranean that were warned of future destruction by both Isaiah and Ezekiel. Over the centuries, these cities were threatened and then dominated by the same adversaries, the Assyrians and Babylonians, who finally ended both the Northern and Southern Kingdoms.

For instance, Isaiah proclaims an oracle against Tyre, warning that the city will be conquered:

> Is this your exultant city
>   whose origin is from days of old,
> whose feet carried her
>   to settle far away?
> Who has planned this
>   against Tyre, the bestower of crowns,
> whose merchants were princes,
>   whose traders were the honored of the earth?
> The Lord of hosts has planned it—
>   to defile the pride of all glory,
>   to shame all the honored of the earth. (Isa 23:7–9)

Ezekiel, too, warns the king of Tyre of coming disaster:

Because your heart is proud
 and you have said "I am a god."...
Because you compare your mind
 with the mind of a god,
therefore, I will bring strangers against you,
 the most terrible of nations;
they shall draw their swords against the
 beauty of your wisdom
and defile your splendor. (Ezek 28:2b, 6b–7)

Next, Ezekiel warns Sidon against coming disaster:

The word of the LORD came to me: Mortal, set your face toward Sidon, and prophesy against it, and say, Thus says the Lord GOD:

I am against you, O Sidon,
 and I will gain glory in your midst.
They shall know that I am the LORD
 when I execute judgments in it,
 and manifest my holiness in it;
for I will send pestilence into it,
 and bloodshed into its streets;
and the dead shall fall in its midst,
 by the sword that is against it on every side.
 (Ezek 28:20–23)

Jesus also compares the unreceptive and unrepentant cities of Chorazin and Bethsaida to Sodom, an allusion to the Book of Genesis (Gen 19:1–29) and the destruction of Sodom and Gomorrah that we discussed in our last chapter. Jesus says: "For if the deeds of power done in you had been done in Sodom, it would have remained until this day. But I tell you that on the day of judgment it will be more tolerable for the land of Sodom than for you" (Matt 11:23b–24).

KEEPING THE SABBATH

Jesus's next two controversies involve questions about keeping the Sabbath. Keeping the Sabbath was central to Jewish identity and had been for over a thousand years. To keep holy the Sabbath is one of the Ten Commandments that God gave Moses on Mount Sinai. God says to Moses: "Remember the sabbath day, and keep it holy. Six days you shall labor and do all your work. But the seventh day is a sabbath to the LORD your God; you shall not do any work—you, your son or your daughter, your male or female slave, your livestock, or the alien resident in your towns. For in six days the LORD made heaven and earth, the sea, and all that is in them, but rested the seventh day; therefore the LORD blessed the sabbath day and consecrated it" (Exod 20:8–11). Even God observes the Sabbath.

The Book of Deuteronomy repeats the same fourth commandment, but gives a different reason for keeping the Sabbath, a humanitarian reason. When naming all the people who are to rest, Deuteronomy says:

> But the seventh day is a sabbath to the LORD your God; you shall not do any work—you, or your son or your daughter, or your male or female slave, or your ox or your donkey, or any of your livestock, or the resident alien in your town, so that your male and female slave may rest as well as you. Remember that you were a slave in the land of Egypt, and the LORD your God brought you out from there with a mighty hand and an outstretched arm; therefore the LORD your God commanded you to keep the sabbath day. (Deut 5:14–15)

The Israelites know what it is to be mistreated as a slave and a foreigner because of their four hundred years in Egypt. They are never to mistreat others in the same way (see also Exod 23:12–13).

Matthew tells us that Jesus's disciples were hungry as they walked through the grainfields on the Sabbath, and so they plucked some heads of grain and ate them. The Pharisees confronted Jesus, accusing his disciples of doing something that was not lawful on the Sabbath. Jesus responds by challenging the Pharisees: "Have you not read what David did when he and his companions were hungry? He entered the house of God and ate the bread of the Presence, which it was not lawful for him or his companions to eat, but only for the priests" (Matt 12:3–4).

With this response, Jesus was assuming that the Pharisees had read both 1 Samuel and Leviticus. First Samuel 21 tells the story to which Jesus refers. David comes to the priest, Ahimelech, explains that he is on a secret mission for Saul, and asks for food that he can take to his men. The priest says, "I have no ordinary bread at hand, only holy bread" (1 Sam 21:4). We learn what the holy bread is in the Book of Leviticus. Each Sabbath the priest was to put out twelve loaves, standing for the twelve tribes, in the tent of meeting. Only the priest was to eat the bread (see Lev 24:8–9). Jesus is arguing that there is precedent in Scripture for doing something forbidden if people are hungry and need to be fed.

Jesus's second argument to the Pharisees is based on an instruction given to priests in the Book of Numbers. Jesus says, "Or have you not read in the law that on the sabbath the priests in the temple break the sabbath and yet are guiltless?" (Matt 12:5). Numbers says, "On the sabbath day: two male lambs a year old without blemish, and two-tenths of an ephah of choice flour for a grain offering, mixed with oil, and its drink offering—this is the burnt offering for every sabbath, in addition to the regular burnt offering and its drink offering" (Num 28:9–10). So, priests, as part of their sacred duty, were required to work on the sabbath. This worship of God and service to the community took priority over the sabbath regulations.

Jesus next says, "But if you had known what this means, 'I desire mercy and not sacrifice,' you would not have condemned the guiltless. For the Son of Man is Lord of the sabbath" (Matt 12:7–8). This is the second time Jesus has quoted this passage from Hosea 6:6. He quoted the same passage in Matthew 9:13 when the Pharisees challenged him for dining with tax collectors and sinners. It is hard for the Pharisees, who are legalists, to understand that love and mercy are Jesus's priorities. Jesus then makes a statement that would have been astounding and disturbing to the Pharisees. Once more referring to himself as the "Son of Man," the allusion to the Book of Daniel, Jesus claims that he is "Lord of the Sabbath." Who, in heaven's name, is Jesus claiming to be?

The argument between Jesus and the Pharisees about what is legal to do on the Sabbath continues as Jesus enters the synagogue and encounters a man with a withered hand. The Pharisees challenge Jesus, asking, "Is it lawful to cure on the sabbath?" (Matt 12:10). Their motive for asking is not to learn from Jesus, but to gather evidence against him. Jesus does not avoid their challenge, but challenges them right back, illustrating that Jesus knows the law just as well as they do. Jesus says, "Suppose one of you has only one sheep and it falls into a pit on the sabbath; will you not lay hold of it and lift it out? How much more valuable is a human being than a sheep! So it is lawful to do good on the sabbath" (Matt 12:11–12).

The Pharisees couldn't argue the point. They, too, knew what Deuteronomy teaches about withholding help if a neighbor's ox, sheep, or donkey wanders away or needs help: "You shall not see your neighbor's donkey or ox fallen on the road and ignore it; you shall help to lift it up" (Deut 22:4). Jesus is arguing, based on the law, that not to help a person in need is against the law whether or not it is the sabbath. Jesus then cures the man with the withered hand. The fact that Jesus has the power to cure the man's hand adds authority to his claim that the "Son of Man is Lord of the sabbath" (Matt 12:8). The Pharisees are not persuaded. Rather, they are angered to the point of wanting to destroy Jesus.

When Jesus became aware of the Pharisees' intentions, he left. However, he did not stop healing. In order not to anger his enemies more, Jesus ordered those he healed not to make him known. Matthew then tells us, "This was to fulfill what had been spoken though the prophet Isaiah:

> Here is my servant, whom I have chosen,
> my beloved, with whom my soul is well pleased.
> I will put my Spirit upon him,
> and he will proclaim justice to the Gentiles.
> He will not wrangle or cry aloud,
> nor will anyone hear his voice in the streets.
> He will not break a bruised reed
> or quench a smoldering wick
> until he brings justice to victory.
> And in his name the Gentiles will hope. (Matt 12:17–21)

In this, Matthew's eighth fulfillment citation, Matthew is quoting Isaiah 42:1–4, the beginning of Second Isaiah's first Suffering Servant song. As we discussed in chapter 5, the four Suffering Servant songs in Second Isaiah were originally addressed to the exiles in Babylon, giving them hope that God was still with them, and that their suffering had a purpose. The servant in Second Isaiah's servant songs is the nation, Israel, personified. In the context of Matthew's Gospel, the servant is Jesus Christ. As we noted before, the early Church used the Suffering Servant songs to help them understand Jesus, the Messiah, as a Suffering Servant rather than as a conquering, worldly hero.

By reinterpreting Isaiah's Suffering Servant song and applying it to Jesus, Matthew teaches that Jesus is loved by God and chosen by God. Jesus is full of God's Spirit. Jesus will be God's servant to bring the good news of God's love not only to his own people, his fellow Jews, but also to the Gentiles. Jesus will not respond with violence to those who want to destroy him. Rather, he will continue to heal, he will continue to teach love and compassion, and he will persevere until his mission has been completed.

This fulfillment citation also serves to set the stage for Jesus's next controversy with the Pharisees. This controversy, too, centers our attention on Jesus's identity as the Messiah, the Son of David, the Son of Man. Jesus heals a demoniac. This causes the crowds to ask, "Can this be the Son of David?" (Matt 12:23). Remember how significant that title is to Matthew's Gospel and to Matthew's audience. The Pharisees come to the opposite conclusion. They think that Jesus's power comes from Satan, God's enemy, not from God. Matthew's audience, of course, has just been taught, through the reinterpretation of Second Isaiah's Suffering Servant song, that Jesus has power because God's Spirit is upon him.

Jesus argues that a kingdom divided against itself cannot stand. His power is from God. Jesus says, "But if it is by the Spirit of God that I cast out demons, then the kingdom of God has come to you" (Matt 12:28). Notice the phrase "the kingdom of God." Matthew rarely uses this phrase. Matthew nearly always refers to this reality as "the kingdom of heaven." (Other exceptions are in Matt 19:24 and in Matt 21:31, 43). As we read Jesus's third sermon, a sermon about the kingdom of God/heaven (Matt 13:1–52), we will see that Matthew usually calls this kingdom the kingdom of heaven even though his source, Mark, uses the phrase "the kingdom of God." Scripture scholars surmise that Matthew does this out of sensitivity to his Jewish audience, who refrain from naming God out of respect and awe for God's holiness.

Jesus then makes a puzzling statement. He says, "Whoever speaks a word against the Son of Man will be forgiven, but whoever speaks against the Holy Spirit will not be forgiven, either in this age or in the age to come" (Matt 12:12). Jesus is once more claiming to be the "Son of Man," the apocalyptic figure whom the Book of Daniel pictures as coming at the end time on the clouds of heaven. Why would blasphemy against the Son of Man be forgiven, but not blasphemy against the Holy Spirit? Scripture scholars debate the answer to this question, and no answer seems completely satisfactory. One suggestion is that a sincere person could fail to recognize Jesus, the Son of Man, but later understand, repent, and become Jesus's disciple. A person who rejects the Holy Spirit has rejected the very source of truth and understanding. That person remains unreceptive to truth, never repents, and so never receives the forgiveness that is always offered to a repentant sinner.

Jesus then accuses the Pharisees of being a "brood of vipers." Jesus says, "You brood of vipers! How can you speak good things, when you are evil? For out of the abundance of the heart the mouth speaks. The good person brings good things out of a good treasure, and the evil person brings evil things out of an evil treasure" (Matt 12:34–35). Here Jesus is applying the wisdom learned in Proverbs to his adversaries. In Proverbs we read:

> The thoughts of the righteous are just;
>   the advice of the wicked is treacherous.
> The words of the wicked are a deadly ambush,
>   but the speech of the upright delivers them.
>   (Prov 12:5, 6)

Not to be deterred, the Pharisees and scribes ask Jesus for a sign. In answer, Jesus continues to allude to the Old Testament, this time to the Books of Jonah and 1 Kings.

THE SIGN OF JONAH

In response to the Pharisee's request for a sign, Jesus refers first to the Book of Jonah, saying:

> An evil and adulterous generation asks for a sign, but no sign will be given to it except the sign of the prophet Jonah. For just as Jonah was three days and three nights in the belly of the sea monster, so for three days and three nights the Son of Man will be in the heart of the earth. The people of Nineveh will rise up at the judgment with this generation and condemn it, because they repented at the proclamation of Jonah, and see, something greater than Jonah is here! (Matt 12:39–41)

The Book of Jonah appears with the books of the prophets in both the Jewish and Christian Scriptures, but Jonah is a different kind of writing from any of the prophetic books we have discussed so far, books like Ezekiel and Isaiah. The book's literary form is didactic fiction, that is, it tells a fictional story that teaches an important lesson: God loves even our political enemies. The author is writing his story after the Babylonian exile. His fellow Jews are getting settled back in Judah and are not always being welcomed by the people already living there. The author is teaching his readers that they must not consider those who are resistant to them as enemies. Rather they should be witnesses of God's love to all those they meet, whether fellow Jew or not.

The story is set much earlier than when it was written, when Assyria was threatening the Northern Kingdom. In the story, God tells Jonah to go and preach to the Ninevites. Nineveh was the capital of Assyria, and so represents the enemy. Jonah doesn't want to go, not because, like other historical prophets, he feels unworthy or too young. Jonah doesn't want to go because he doesn't want the Ninevites to be saved. He wants them to be destroyed. So, he runs away, gets thrown off a ship when a storm arises, gets swallowed by a large fish, experiences a conversion while in the belly of the fish for three days, gets vomited out by the fish, goes to Nineveh, and announces, "Forty days more, and

Nineveh shall be overthrown" (Jonah 3:4). Lo and behold, everyone in the city hears Jonah's words and repents. All put on sackcloth, even the animals. "When God saw what they did, how they turned from their evil ways, God changed his mind about the calamity that he had said he would bring upon them; and he did not do it" (Jonah 3:10).

You would think that Jonah would be overjoyed. He had been God's instrument to save a great city! However, Jonah has the opposite reaction. He is angry with God for this change of mind. He wanted the city destroyed. God then reproaches Jonah for his lack of love. God reminds Jonah that God created the Ninevites. God says, "Should I not be concerned about Nineveh, that great city, in which there are more than a hundred and twenty thousand persons who do not know their right hand from their left, and also many animals?" (Jonah 4:11). The author obviously has a sense of humor and understands why it is hard to love your adversaries. Nevertheless, the author is teaching that everyone who exists is a beloved child of God, even those who are not part of our group, and we are to learn to treat them lovingly too.

The lesson taught in the Book of Jonah is a perfect example of how the overarching narrative of Scripture that we discussed in chapter 4 reveals a growing knowledge of the ramifications of the belief that God is love. Remember that the Israelites learned this truth over centuries. Early in their history, the Israelites understood that God loved them, but they did not understand that God loved other nations, too. However, events allowed them to grow in their understanding of God's love. The Babylonian exile ended because Cyrus, who was a Persian, conquered the Babylonians and allowed the exiles in Babylon to return to the promised land. Therefore, Cyrus was seen as a messiah, an anointed one, by the Israelites because they understood him to be God's instrument in saving them, God's instrument in keeping God's covenant promises to them.

In Isaiah 45 we read:

> Thus says the LORD to his anointed, to Cyrus.
> whose right hand I have grasped
> to subdue nations before him
> and strip kings of their robes,

to open doors before him—
  and the gates shall not be closed....
For the sake of my servant Jacob,
  and Israel my chosen,
I call you by your name,
  I surname you, though you do not know me.
I am the LORD, and there is no other. (Isa 45:1, 4–5a)

This event caused the Israelites to realize that if God called Cyrus and used him as God's instrument to save God's chosen people, God must love Cyrus. Therefore, God must love other nations too. This is the profound truth taught by the author of Jonah. God does love other nations, not only those who have freed Israel but also those who have been Israel's adversaries, including Assyria and the people of Nineveh.

As we have already learned from Jesus's Sermon on the Mount, Jesus fully embraced this teaching when he taught his disciples to love not only their friends but also their enemies. However, by alluding to the Book of Jonah, Jesus uses Jonah's three days in the belly of the fish as a type, as a foreshadowing, of his own future three days in the tomb.

FIRST KINGS

Jesus continues his response to the Pharisees who have asked for a sign by saying, "The queen of the South will rise up at the judgment with this generation and condemn it, because she came from the ends of the earth to listen to the wisdom of Solomon, and see, something greater than Solomon is here!" (Matt 12:42). When Jesus claims that not only the people of Nineveh but also the queen of the South will rise up in judgment on the present generation, Jesus is referring to a story in 1 Kings. The first chapters of 1 Kings give us an account of Israel as King David dies and his successor, Solomon, succeeds him. King Solomon is famous for building the Temple in Jerusalem and for bringing the ark of the covenant into the Temple. He is also famous for his wisdom. The author of 1 Kings says: "God gave Solomon very great wisdom, discernment, and breadth of understanding as vast as the sand on the seashore, so that Solomon's wisdom surpassed the wisdom of all the people of the east, and all the wisdom of Egypt. He was wiser than anyone else...his fame spread throughout all the surrounding nations" (1 Kgs 4:29–31).

We read the story of the queen of the South (the queen of Sheba) in 1 Kings 10:1–13 "When the queen of Sheba heard of the fame of Solomon (fame due to the name of the LORD), she came to test him with hard questions." Solomon welcomed the queen and answered all her questions. The queen was extremely grateful. "So she said to the king, 'The report was true that I heard in my own land of your accomplishments and of your wisdom, but I did not believe the reports until I came and my own eyes had seen it. Not even half had been told me; your wisdom and prosperity far surpass the report that I had heard'" (1 Kgs 10:6–7).

In comparing his contemporary generation to Nineveh and the queen of Sheba, Jesus is reproaching those who, like those Pharisees who are plotting against him, refuse to have an open mind to learning new truths and who refuse to repent once they recognize their errors and their sins. An open mind, a willingness to grow in one's understanding, and a willingness to repent of one's failures are necessary in order to welcome the Son of Man and his teachings. Truly, Jesus, the Son of Man, is greater than Solomon.

After giving his dire warnings against his contemporary generation and declaring that those who do God's will have a bond even closer than family relationships, Jesus begins his third discourse, teaching about the kingdom of heaven. This discourse, too, contains Old Testament allusions including fulfillment citations and Son of Man references.

"PARABLES" ABOUT THE KINGDOM OF HEAVEN

As Jesus teaches a large crowd and his disciples about the kingdom of heaven, his teachings are consistently called "parables." However, two of the parables, the parable of the sower (Matt 13:3–9) and the parable of the weeds among the wheat (Matt 13:24–30), are later interpreted as allegories (see Matt 13:18–23, 36–43). The word *parable* is also used to name what are extended similes. Since understanding literary form is essential to understanding Scripture, we will first define *parable*, *allegory*, and *simile*, then explain why the English translation of Matthew's Gospel uses the word *parable* to name all three.

To teach through parables was part of Jesus's Jewish heritage. A parable is a story told to a particular audience that has the purpose of calling that audience to self-awareness and conversion. The parable fulfills this function by interesting the listeners in the story line, having a plot element in the story that compares to the listeners—one with whom the listeners can identify—and then having that comparison lead the listeners to hear the call to conversion. In other words, to teach through parables is to try to get around people's defense mechanisms so that they can hear a message that they may not want to hear.

A perfect example of the literary form *parable* appears in 2 Samuel. The person telling the parable is the prophet Nathan. The person to whom the parable is being told is King David. King David was a great king. He united the twelve tribes into one nation. His contemporaries understood him as God's instrument to fulfill God's promises to Abraham. However, David was also a great sinner. He committed adultery with a soldier's wife, Bathsheba. She became pregnant, and to hide the sin, David had her husband sent to the front lines and so he was killed in battle. It was the prophet's job to remind the king who was king and to call David to repentance. To do this, Nathan tells David a parable:

> There were two men in a certain city, the one rich and the other poor. The rich man had very many flocks and herds; but the poor man had nothing but one little ewe lamb, which he had bought. He brought it up, and it grew up with him and with his children; it used to eat of his meager fare, and drink from his cup, and lie in his bosom, and it was like a daughter to him. Now there came a traveler to the rich man, and he was loath to take one of his own flock or herd to prepare for the wayfarer who had come to him, but he took the poor man's lamb, and prepared that for the guest who had come to him. (2 Sam 12:1–4)

David listened to the story attentively, was outraged with the behavior of the rich man, and said, "As the Lord lives, the man who has done this deserves to die; he shall restore the lamb fourfold, because he did this thing, and because he had no pity" (2 Sam 12:5–6). David has passed judgment on the character in the story, not realizing that he has just passed judgment on himself. Nathan brings the purpose of the parable home: "Nathan said to David, 'You are the man'" (2 Sam 12:7).

We see, then, that to interpret a parable we need to know the person or persons to whom the story is told. Jesus was teaching a resistant audience, to say the least. Jesus is asked why he teaches in parables, and he quotes Isaiah as he answers: "The reason I teach in parables is that 'seeing they do not perceive, and hearing they do not listen, nor do they understand.' With them indeed is fulfilled the prophecy of Isaiah that says:

> You will indeed listen, but never understand,
>   and you will indeed look, but never perceive,
> For this people's heart has grown dull,
>   and their ears are hard of hearing,
>   and they have shut their eyes;
>   so that they might not look with their eyes,
>   and listen with their ears,
> and understand with their heart and turn—
>   and I would heal them. (Matt 13:13–15)

Here Jesus is quoting Isaiah 6:9–10, a passage from Isaiah's call story. Isaiah experiences his call in the Jerusalem Temple around 742 BCE. He is told to preach to those in Judea, the Southern Kingdom, that their sinful behavior has resulted in inevitable suffering. God instructs Isaiah to announce this inevitable suffering by saying:

> Go and say to this people:
> "Keep listening, but do not comprehend;
> keep looking, but do not understand."
> Make the mind of this people dull,
>   and stop their ears,
>   and shut their eyes,
> so that they may not look with their eyes,
>   and listen with their ears,

> and comprehend with their minds,
> And turn and be healed. (Isa 6:9–10)

Like Isaiah, Jesus finds himself preaching to a completely resistant audience. Jesus wants to heal the people, but as long as they are closed to his teaching and intent on destroying him, he cannot heal them.

If one is trying to reach a resistant audience, there is no better method than to teach through parables. As with King David, the listeners get interested in the story, pass judgment on the characters, and realize, only in hindsight, that they have passed judgment on themselves. Scripture scholars believe that we get closest to Jesus's actual words when we are reading the parables.

While understanding the teaching in a parable depends on a single comparison between the audience and something or someone in the story, understanding an allegory depends on a series of comparisons between the literal level of the story and the intended level of the story. Allegories were part of the Greek culture. Scripture scholars surmise that as Jesus's parables were passed on through oral tradition, the social setting in which they were told was not passed on with them. Then, as Gentiles became Christians and started gathering to share Jesus's teachings and to celebrate Eucharist, some of the parables were interpreted as allegories. The allegorical interpretations were then attributed to Jesus and were included in the Gospels.

We can illustrate this two-step process with the parable of the sower (Matt 13:3–8). Jesus tells this parable to a large crowd. A sower sows many seeds. Some fall on the path and are eaten by birds, some get scorched by the sun, some fall in thorns, and some fall on good soil and bear an abundant harvest. As Jesus concludes the parable he says, "Listen anyone with ears, listen!" Jesus obviously feels urgency about his message. He is comparing his audience to the good soil and is begging them to become good soil too.

Later Matthew includes an allegorical interpretation of the parable and attributes it to Jesus (Matt 13:18–23). Here the seeds are compared to people who hear the word of the kingdom in various settings and do not receive it. They do not bear fruit. Those who do receive the word of the kingdom bear much fruit. The allegory does not correct and call to conversion a particular audience, as does the parable. People could listen to the allegorical interpretation and think that it applies to many other people but avoid applying the lesson to themselves.

Matthew's Gospel also refers to what are really extended similes as parables. A simile is a comparison that uses the words *like* or *as.* Jesus teaches that the kingdom of heaven is like a mustard seed (13:31), like a hidden treasure that is found (13:44), like a fine pearl that is found (Matt 13:45), and like a net that is thrown into the sea and catches fish of every kind (Matt 13:47).

One might well ask, "Why are allegories and similes all called parables in the Gospel, and why does it matter?" Hebrew, the language in which the Jewish Scripture was originally written, had a single word, *masal,* that referred to a number of different kinds of sayings, parables included. The Hebrew Scripture was translated into Greek in the third century BCE. This was because the Hellenistic culture was becoming predominant, and many Jews were speaking Greek rather than Hebrew. In the Greek translation, the Septuagint, the Hebrew word for a variety of sayings was translated as *parable,* a word that entered English through Latin. Matthew's Gospel was originally written in Greek Koine, so he used the word parable to refer to a variety of sayings that make comparisons, as does our English translation.

The reason distinguishing parables from allegories is important is that, while some parables can be allegorized and still teach something true, that is not always the case. For instance, later in Matthew's Gospel we will read the parable of the talents (Matt 25:14–30). In this story, a master entrusts money to three slaves, leaves town, and when he returns, asks the slaves for an accounting of their stewardship. Two made profits. The third did not. The master is angry with the slave for not earning interest on a loan, a practice considered sinful at the time, and throws him out, saying, "As for this worthless slave, throw him into the outer darkness, where there will be weeping and gnashing of teeth" (Matt 25:30). If one were to allegorize this parable, one would come away with a frightening image of God. Matthew is not implying that this mean master stands for God.

Matthew is revealing something about Jesus's identity and the truth of Jesus's teachings when Matthew says, "Jesus told the crowds all these things in parables; without a parable he told them nothing. This was to fulfill what had been spoken through the prophet: 'I will open my mouth to speak in parables; / I will proclaim what has been hidden from the foundation of the world'" (Matt 13:34–35).

In this fulfillment citation Matthew is quoting Psalm 78:2. The psalmist says:

> Give ear, O my people, to my teaching:
> incline your ears to the words of my mouth.
> I will open my mouth in a parable;
> I will utter dark sayings from of old,
> things that we have heard and known,
> that our ancestors have told us.
> We will not hide them from their children;
> we will tell to the coming generation
> the glorious deeds of the LORD, and his might,
> and the wonders that he had done. (Ps 78:1–4)

Matthew is teaching that Jesus is the one who knows what has been hidden from the foundation of the word, who can truly reveal God's wondrous deeds.

THE KINGDOM OF HEAVEN

What is Matthew teaching his fellow Jews (and us) about the kingdom of heaven through Jesus's third discourse? In the parable of the sower, he is exhorting his contemporaries to be receptive to Jesus's teachings, to be good soil. Only then can they enter God's kingdom. In the parable of the weeds among the wheat, he explains that the coming of the kingdom is a process that requires patience and tolerance on their part. They are not to destroy their adversaries.

In the allegorical interpretation of the parable of the weeds among the wheat, Jesus says:

> The one who sows the good seed is the Son of Man; the field is the world, and the good seed are the children of the

> kingdom; the weeds are the children of the evil one, and the enemy who sowed them is the devil; the harvest is the end of the age, and the reapers are angels. Just as the weeds are collected and burned up with fire, so will it be at the end of the age. The Son of Man will send his angels, and they will collect out of his kingdom all causes of sin and all evildoers. (Matt 13:37–41)

This passage would have been important for many in Matthew's audience since Matthew is claiming that Jesus is the Son of Man who will come at the end time and finally, fully establish his kingdom.

In comparing the kingdom of heaven to a mustard seed and to yeast, Matthew is once more showing that the kingdom is both present and future. In comparing the kingdom to a hidden treasure and a fine pearl, he is teaching that once discovered, the kingdom becomes one's top priority, more valuable than anything else on earth. In comparing the kingdom to a net that catches fish of every kind, both good and bad, he is once more explaining that the coming of the kingdom is a process and that the good will be separated from the bad at the end time. Patience is required.

At the end of Jesus's third discourse Jesus asks, "Have you understood all this?" (Matt 13:51). Matthew assures his fellow Jews that they can be faithful to their two-thousand-year covenant with God and, at the same time, be open to learning what Jesus is teaching by picturing Jesus saying, "Therefore every scribe who has been trained for the kingdom of heaven is like the master of a household who brings out of his treasure what is new and what is old" (Matt 13:52). The Books of Isaiah, Daniel, and Psalms are old, but Matthew still quotes and alludes to them as he persuades his fellow Jews to be open to what is new, the son of David and the Son of Man, Jesus Christ, who is inviting them into the kingdom of heaven.

7

GROWING ANIMOSITY AND LESSONS ON LOVE

As Matthew begins his fourth section, comprised of a narrative about Jesus (Matt 13:53—17:27) and a discourse by Jesus (Matt 18:1–35), Matthew continues his Old Testament allusions, sometimes explicitly and sometimes more subtly. While no stories of Jesus's mighty acts end with a fulfillment citation, the stories would definitely have caused Matthew's fellow Jews to recall important events in their Scriptures, accounts of God's mighty acts in the lives of their ancestors. In this section we will see that resistance to Jesus and his teachings is growing, and that Jesus gives his disciples instructions on how to live in fidelity to Jesus's gospel of love.

First, Matthew tells us that Jesus goes to his hometown synagogue and teaches the people. They are astounded by Jesus's wisdom and acts of power, but instead of being open to Jesus's message, they take offense at him. Jesus remarks, "Prophets are not without honor except in their own country and in their own house" (Matt 13:57). As we discussed in our last chapter, it is because of people's lack of receptivity that Jesus so often teaches in parables. He is trying to get around people's resistance to hearing the truth as he calls them to self-knowledge and conversion.

Jesus was becoming so well known that Herod Antipas, the then ruler of Galilee, had heard of him. Herod Antipas is not the same Herod as Herod the Great, whom we met in Matthew's infancy narrative. *Herod* is the family name of the men who had control in Palestine from the middle of the first century BCE to the middle of the first century CE under Roman rule. Herod Antipas was Herod the Great's son. Matthew tells us that Herod Antipas had concluded that Jesus "is John the Baptist; he has been raised from the dead, and for this reason these powers are at work in him" (Matt 14:2).

Matthew then tells us that Herod Antipas had previously arrested John the Baptist because John the Baptist had told him that it was not lawful for Herod to marry his brother's wife while his brother was still alive. That is adultery. The Book of Leviticus teaches this clearly. In chapter 20 we read, "If a man commits adultery with the wife of his neighbor, both the adulterer and the adulteress shall be put to death; If a man takes his brother's wife, it is impurity" (Lev 20:10, 21). It is no wonder that Herod feared John the Baptist and wanted him silenced, and that his wife, Herodias, wanted John the Baptist dead. That is why she asked her daughter to ask Herod for John's head on a platter.

Another interesting element of this story is that it reveals that Herod himself had come to consider the possibility that there is life after death. In Jesus's time, some Jews believed in life after death, and some did not. We read of this division in the Acts of the Apostles when Paul is defending himself before a Jewish council:

> When Paul noticed that some were Sadducees and others were Pharisees, he called out in the council, "Brothers, I am a Pharisee, a son of Pharisees. I am on trial concerning the hope of the resurrection of the dead." When he said this, a dissension began between the Pharisees and the Sadducees, and the assembly was divided. (The Sadducees say that there is no resurrection, or angel or spirit; but the Pharisees acknowledge all three.) (Acts 23:6–9)

The idea that there might be life after death appears in the Book of Wisdom, a book that was originally written in Greek in the first century

BCE by a faithful Jew living in Alexandria, Egypt. This book is in the Catholic and Orthodox Old Testaments and in the Septuagint, the Greek version of the Jewish Scriptures. However, it is not in the canon of other Christians or in the Hebrew Scriptures. Greek-speaking Jews, such as Matthew's readers in Antioch, Syria, would have been familiar with this book. The book is also called the *Wisdom of Solomon* because the author attributes the book to Solomon, who, as we know, was renowned for his wisdom.

The author of Wisdom used reason to arrive at his belief in life after death. He thought that God is too loving to allow the fate of a good person and the fate of an evil person to be the same. Wisdom teaches:

> But the souls of the righteous are in the hand of God,
> and no torment will ever touch them.
> In the eyes of the foolish they seemed to have died,
> and their departure was thought to be a disaster,
> and their going from us to be their destruction;
> but they are at peace.
> For though in the sight of others they were punished,
> their hope is full of immortality.
> Having been disciplined a little, they will receive great good,
> because God tested them and found them worthy of himself.
> (Wis 3:1–5)

That some Jews had come to believe in life after death is important because it affects their understanding of the words *messiah* and *kingdom*. As the belief in life after death developed, the role of a messiah and the meaning of the words the *kingdom of God* as compared to the *kingdom of David* were redefined. This growth in understanding would be absolutely necessary in order to come to a belief that Jesus is the hoped for Messiah—Jesus, who, instead of freeing his people from Roman rule and establishing a kingdom on earth, was killed by the Romans. As we have already noted, Matthew pictures Jesus expanding his disciples' idea of the *kingdom* when he teaches them to pray, "Your kingdom come. Your will be done, on earth as it is in heaven" (Matt 6:10) and when he consistently refers to Jesus as both *the son of David* and *the Son of Man*.

THE MULTIPLICATION OF THE LOAVES

Matthew's Gospel gives two separate accounts of Jesus multiplying loaves to feed hungry people: the feeding of the five thousand, not counting women and children (Matt 14:13–21), and the feeding of the four thousand, not counting women and children (Matt 15:32–39). While these stories do not explicitly quote Scripture, they evoke memories of two Old Testament stories: God feeding God's people with manna in the desert (Exod 16) and Elisha multiplying twenty loaves of barley and some ears of grain to feed one hundred people (2 Kgs 4:42–44).

First, when Jesus multiplies the loaves and fishes for the five thousand, it is evening, the crowds are hungry, and they are in a deserted place. The disciples suggest sending the crowds away to fend for themselves. However, Jesus has compassion on them and tells the disciples to feed the crowd themselves. They object. How can they? They have only five loaves and two fish. Jesus has the crowd sit down. He then "blessed and broke the loaves, and gave them to the disciples, and the disciples gave them to the crowds. And all ate and were filled; and they took up what was left over of the broken pieces, twelve baskets full" (Matt 14:19b–20).

The feeding of the four thousand is similar. Jesus has compassion on the crowd and wants to feed them. They are in a deserted place. The disciples ask, "Where are we to get enough bread in the desert to feed so great a crowd?" (Matt 15:33). This time the disciples have seven loaves and a few fish. Once more, Jesus has the crowd sit down, he blesses and breaks the loaves and gives them to the disciples to give to the crowd. After the crowd has eaten, there are seven baskets of broken pieces left over.

What is Matthew teaching by including two such similar stories in his Gospel? In each story, Jesus is the one who wants to feed the crowd, and after he multiplies the loaves and fish, he gives the food to the disciples to distribute to the people. Matthew is teaching that Jesus's disciples are always to feed God's hungry people. The number of leftover baskets is also significant: Twelve recalls the twelve tribes and the twelve apostles. There is enough for the whole Church. Seven represents fullness, completeness. There is enough for all the people. Also, in each story, the blessing and breaking of the bread is eucharistic language and foreshadows the Last Supper. Matthew's message here is that God continues to feed God's people through the Eucharist.

However, the stories do not only foreshadow the Last Supper, but they also recall Old Testament stories of God feeding God's hungry people. Foremost among these stories is God providing the Israelites manna in the desert (see Exod 16). In that story, too, God has compassion on God's people. God has heard their complaining about their hunger, and God provides them manna in the desert. God tells Moses to say to them, "At twilight you shall eat meat, and in the morning, you shall have your fill of bread; then you shall know that I am the LORD your God" (Exod 16:12). When the Israelites discovered the manna, they did not know what it was. Moses said, "It is the bread that the LORD has given you to eat" (Exod 16:15b). The Israelites ate manna for forty years. All subsequent generations thanked, celebrated, and honored God for feeding their ancestors in the desert.

The stories of the multiplication of loaves also recall a story in 2 Kings about Elisha, the prophet who followed Elijah. The author of 2 Kings tells us that a man brought Elisha "twenty loaves of barley and fresh ears of grain in his sack. Elisha said, 'Give it to the people and let them eat.' But his servant said, 'How can I set this before a hundred people?' So, he repeated, 'Give it to the people and let them eat, for thus says the LORD, "They shall eat and have some left."' He set it before them, they ate, and had some left, according to the word of the LORD" (2 Kgs 4:42–44).

The similarities between this story and Matthew's stories are obvious. The dialogue between Elisha and the man who brought the food is similar to Jesus's dialogues with his disciples. In all three stories, the people eat, are satisfied, and have food left. In all three stories, it is the Lord who has provided. Through these allusions to Exodus and 2 Kings, Matthew is teaching that Jesus is the Lord who provides bread for his people.

JESUS WALKS ON WATER

In his next story, Matthew portrays Jesus as the Lord who can walk on water and calm the wind (see Matt 14:22–23). The disciples are in a boat. There is a high wind. Jesus comes to join them by walking on the water. They are terrified and think he is a ghost. Jesus says, "Take heart, it is I; do not be afraid" (Matt 14:27). Peter's response once more turns our attention to Jesus's identity. Peter says, "Lord, if it is you, command me to come to you on the water" (Matt 14:28). Notice that Peter calls Jesus "Lord." Jesus invites Peter to come. Peter starts to walk toward Jesus on the water but, because of the strong wind, becomes afraid and starts to sink. Jesus saves Peter, they get into the boat, and the wind ceases. Matthew concludes the story by saying, "And those in the boat worshipped him, saying, 'Truly you are the Son of God'" (Matt 14:33).

This is the second time in Matthew's Gospel when Jesus is pictured as having control over the wind and the sea. In chapter 5, when discussing Jesus calming the storm (see Matt 8:23–27), we explained the form of a miracle story and said that this story alludes to Psalm 107. That earlier story, like this story of Jesus walking on water, concludes by centering our attention on the identity of Jesus. However, Psalm 107 is not the only Old Testament text that pictures God being worshipped, praised, and thanked for saving God's people and by having authority over the seas.

In Psalm 77 we read:

> I will call to mind the deeds of the Lord;
>   I will remember your wonders of old.
> I will meditate on all your work,
>   and muse on your mighty deeds.
> Your way, O God, is holy.
>   What god is so great as our God?
> You are the God who works wonders;
>   you have displayed your might among the peoples.
> With your strong arm you redeemed your people,
>   the descendants of Jacob and Joseph.
>
> When the waters saw you, O God,
>   when the waters saw you, they were afraid;
>   the very deep trembled.
> The clouds poured out water;
>   the skies thundered;
>   your arrows flashed on every side.

The crash of your thunder was in the whirlwind;
your lightnings lit up the world;
the earth trembled and shook.
Your way was through the sea,
your path, through the mighty waters;
yet your footprints were unseen.
You led your people like a flock
by the hand of Moses and Aaron. (Ps 77:11–20)

Jesus's authority over the water and the wind has the same effect on the disciples that God's parting of the waters to save his people at the time of the exodus had on the author of Psalm 77: wonder, awe, and worship. This time the disciples do not say, "What sort of man is this, that even the winds and the sea obey him?" (Matt 8:27), as they did when Jesus calmed the storm. This time, Matthew tells us that "those in the boat worshipped him, saying, 'Truly you are the Son of God'" (Matt 14:33).

CONTROVERSIES AND CURES

After healing many, Jesus once again finds himself challenged by the Pharisees and scribes. This time the argument is over ritual purity. The Pharisees and the scribes want to know why Jesus's disciples do not wash their hands before eating as tradition requires. Jesus contrasts rules that have developed over years and have become tradition—tradition that the legalistic Pharisees consider all important—to God's commandments. In doing so, Jesus makes it clear that he knows Torah, the Law, just as well as his opponents do.

Scripture does not picture God saying, "Wash your hands before you eat!" That is a rule that became part of later tradition. Jesus faithfully quotes the Old Testament when he reminds the Pharisees and scribes that God did say, "Honor your father and your mother," and, "Whoever speaks evil of father or mother must surely die" (Matt 15:4). One of the Ten Commandments that God gave Moses was, "Honor your father and your mother, so that your days may be long in the land that the LORD your God is giving you" (Exod 20:12). Leviticus teaches, "All who curse father or mother shall be put to death; having cursed father or mother, their blood is upon them" (Lev 20:9).

Jesus then accuses the Pharisees and scribes of following a tradition that causes them to disobey the commandment to honor their fathers and mothers. Jesus says, "But you say that whoever tells father or mother, 'Whatever support you might have had from me is given to God,' then that person need not honor the father. So, for the sake of your tradition, you make void the word of God" (Matt 15:5–6). The tradition to which Jesus is referring involved taking a vow in which a person promises to give a gift to God. So, the gift has been "given to God." If keeping that vow meant that a person could no longer honor his parents, the Pharisees considered keeping the vow more important than obeying the commandment. That is why Jesus accuses them of honoring their tradition, thereby "making void the word of God" (Matt 15:6).

Jesus then once more quotes the prophet Isaiah. Jesus says, "You hypocrites! Isaiah prophesied rightly about you when he said: 'This people honors me with their lips, / but their hearts are far from me; / in vain do they worship me, / teaching human precepts as doctrines'" (Matt 15:7–9).

In the Book of Isaiah, we read:

> The Lord said:
> Because these people draw near with their mouths
>   and honor me with their lips,
>   while their hearts are far from me,
> and their worship of me is a human commandment learned
>   by rote;
> so I will again do
>   amazing things with this people,
>   shocking and amazing.
> The wisdom of their wise shall perish,
>   and the discernment of the discerning shall be hidden.
>   (Isa 29:13–14)

The setting for this prophecy of First Isaiah (742–701 BCE) is Judah, the Southern Kingdom, when it was being threatened by the

Syro-Ephraimite alliance. Isaiah was imploring the king, Ahaz, to trust God and God's covenant promises, not political alliances, in order to avoid being conquered. Instead, King Ahaz allowed Judah to become a vassal state of Assyria. Isaiah prophesies that true wisdom will remain hidden from the people because they refuse to listen and learn God's ways.

In quoting this passage, Jesus accuses his critics of acting just as Ahaz and the leaders of Judah did. They are refusing to listen to God's words and be moved by them. Their hearts are far from God. They are hypocrites, not wise leaders.

Jesus then addresses the crowd, not just the Pharisees. However, his next comment enrages the Pharisees even more. Jesus tells the crowd, "It is not what goes into the mouth that defiles a person, but it is what comes out of the mouth that defiles" (Matt 15:11). While washing hands before eating was a tradition, but not in Torah, instructions about clean and unclean food are in the Law. We discussed purity laws earlier when talking about Jesus touching a leper. Purity laws also involved instructions about not eating certain foods. Chapter 11 of Leviticus lists the animals, the fish, and the birds that are clean and unclean. God tells Moses to admonish the Israelites that to eat what is unclean should be detestable to them.

While Jesus's teaching about food not making a person unclean seems to declare all food clean, and Mark actually includes that conclusion in his account (see Mark 7:19), Peter obviously does not understand the teaching that way. We know this from the story of Peter and Cornelius that appears in the tenth chapter of the Acts of the Apostles. Peter has a vision in which he "saw the heaven opened and something like a large sheet coming down, being lowered to the ground by its four corners. In it were all kinds of four-footed creatures and reptiles and birds of the air. Then he heard a voice saying, 'Get up, Peter; kill and eat.' 'By no means, Lord; for I have never eaten anything that is profane or unclean.' The voice said to him again, a second time, 'What God has made clean, you must not call profane'" (Acts 10:11–15).

The disciples tell Jesus that the Pharisees took offense at what Jesus said. Jesus responds to this comment in two ways. First, he says that the disciples should not listen to the Pharisees. They are blind guides leading the blind (Matt 15:14). Then, at Peter's request, Jesus elaborates on his teaching. When naming what comes out of a person that defiles that person, Jesus refers back to the commandments and the law. "For out of the heart come evil intentions, murder, adultery, fornication, theft, false witness, slander. These are what defile a person, but to eat with unwashed hands does not defile" (Matt 15:19–20).

Once more, accounts of healings follow controversies. Jesus heals the daughter of a Canaanite woman who pleads with Jesus, addressing him as "Lord, Son of David." Jesus tells her that he "was sent only to the lost sheep of the house of Israel" (Matt 15:24). We have already discussed the significance of the oft used title "Son of David" and the phrase "the lost sheep of the house of Israel." Here Jesus is himself following the instructions he gave to his disciples earlier to, "go to the lost sheep of the house of Israel" (Matt 10:6). The fact that he himself responds to the woman's great faith by healing her daughter shows once again that Jesus was not excluding Gentiles; he was saying that the disciples were to go first to their own people.

As Matthew describes Jesus curing many people, he once more alludes to Isaiah. Matthew says Jesus cured "the lame, the maimed, the blind, the mute, and many others" (Matt 15:30). When Second Isaiah offered hope to the exiles in Babylon that God would be true to God's covenant promises and that they would return to Judah, he described their joy by saying, "Then the eyes of the blind shall be opened, / and the ears of the deaf unstopped; / then the lame shall leap like a deer, / and the tongue of the speechless sing for joy" (Isa 35:5–6). We quoted this passage earlier because Jesus alluded to it when he responded to John the Baptist's question about whether he is the one to come or not. Another passage from Isaiah is just as pertinent:

> On that day the deaf shall hear the words of a scroll,
> and out of their gloom and darkness
> the eyes of the blind shall see.
> The meek shall obtain fresh joy in the LORD,
> and the neediest people shall exult in the Holy One of Israel.
> (Isa 29:18–19)

How ironic it is that after all these acts of power, including the multiplication of the loaves for thousands and the many miracles that fulfilled the words of the prophet Isaiah, the Pharisees and Sadducees ask Jesus once more for a sign. Matthew tells us that they tested Jesus by asking "for a sign from heaven" (Matt 16:1). Jesus points out that they have no trouble reading signs in the sky. They can tell whether the weather will be fair or stormy. Then, with total irony, Jesus says, "No sign will be given it (that is, to this generation) except the sign of Jonah" (Matt 16:4). As we already know, the sign of Jonah is Jesus's resurrection. No generation on earth received more signs, including Jesus's resurrection, than did this generation.

Jesus is exasperated not only with the Pharisees and the Sadducees but also with his disciples. When Jesus warns them to "beware of the yeast of the Pharisees and Sadducees" (Matt 16:6), the disciples do not understand that Jesus is using the word *yeast* as a metaphor for influence. They hear the word *yeast* and think that Jesus is referring to their having forgotten to bring any bread.

To a modern reader, the disciples' misunderstanding seems ridiculous. Why would they understand the phrase *beware of the yeast* not as a metaphor, but literally? The connection between yeast (also called leaven) and bread was obviously strong in the disciples' minds, possibly because they had to *beware of yeast* in bread during their yearly Passover celebration, an occasion that the disciples celebrate with Jesus later in Matthew's Gospel. During Passover, the Jews gratefully remembered God's allowing them to escape their hundreds of years of slavery in Egypt. The ritual included eating only bread without yeast for seven days in order to remember and celebrate their ancestors leaving Egypt in haste, not having time for dough to rise from the effect of yeast. The Book of Exodus gives the following instructions: "Seven days you shall eat unleavened bread, and on the seventh day there shall be a festival to the Lord. Unleavened bread shall be eaten for seven days; no leavened bread shall be seen in your possession, and no leaven shall be seen among you in all your territory" (Exod 13:6–7). The disciples are literally wary of yeast during these yearly celebrations.

Jesus himself does not always associate the word *yeast* with a negative influence. We know this because he earlier compared the coming of the kingdom to the effect of yeast. The effect is gradual, but profound.

When Jesus says *beware of the yeast*, he is warning the disciples against the negative influence of the Jewish leaders who are his adversaries because their effect is also gradual but profound. As we have seen through these controversies, the Sadducees, scribes, and Pharisees are Jesus's main antagonists. The scribes were interpreters of Torah, and most of them also belonged to the religious party called the Pharisees. The Pharisees were middle-class laymen and strict interpreters of Torah. Over the years, they had developed many traditions that they considered just as important as Torah. The Sadducees were nobility; some were priests and some were laymen. They were more political than the Pharisees, but they also interpreted the Law strictly. Pharisees and Sadducees were both members of the Sanhedrin, the Jewish ruling council, but the Sadducees were in the majority, and one of their members was the high priest who led the Sanhedrin. So, in warning his disciples against the influence of the Pharisees and Sadducees, Jesus is warning them against the most powerful and influential ruling body among the Jewish people. As we will soon see, the high priest, Caiaphas, will conspire with the chief priests to have Jesus arrested and killed (see Matt 26:3–4).

WHO IS THE SON OF MAN?

Matthew's next account continues to center the reader's attention on Jesus's identity as the Messiah. Once more, Jesus refers to himself as the "Son of Man" as he questions the disciples. Jesus asks, "'Who do people say that the Son of Man is?' And they said, 'Some say John the Baptist, but others Elijah, and still others Jeremiah or one of the prophets'" (Matt 16:13b–14). Why John the Baptist? John the Baptist, like Jesus, called the people to repentance and announced that the kingdom of heaven had come near (see Matt 3:2). He was then killed by Herod. Why Elijah? Elijah, who went up to heaven in the fiery chariot, was expected to return and prepare for the coming of the Messiah. Why Jeremiah, the prophet in Judah from 627 to 587 BCE, the prophet who went into exile with his people? This question is less easily answered.

We know that naming Jeremiah was important to Matthew because he adds this name to Mark's account of the same story (see Mark 8:27–30). Why? One suggestion is that Matthew is pointing out to his Jewish audience that Jeremiah, like Jesus, was rejected and persecuted by the religious leaders of his own time. In the Book of Jeremiah, we read: "When the officials of Judah heard these things, they came up from the king's house to the house of the LORD, and took their seat in the entry of the New Gate of the house of the LORD. Then the priests and the prophets said to the officials and to all the people, 'This man deserves the sentence of death because he has prophesied against this city, as you have heard with your own ears'" (Jer 26:10–11). Although Jeremiah was not put to death, he was persecuted for teaching an unwelcome truth. Jesus is not the first true prophet who was rejected by his religious leaders and who turned out to be right.

After asking who people say that he is, Jesus asks the disciples, "But who do you say that I am?" (Matt 16:15). In answer to this question, Peter makes his famous declaration of faith, "You are the Messiah, the Son of the living God" (Matt 16:16). Remember that the disciples were still learning just what kind of messiah Jesus would be. They obviously do not understand yet, because when Jesus tells them that he is going to be put to death, Peter rebukes him (see Matt 16:21–23). Peter cannot connect the word *messiah* with someone who is going to be killed. No wonder Jesus warns the disciples "not to tell anyone that he was the Messiah" (Matt 16:20). Jesus does not want them to tell others what they themselves do not yet understand.

When Jesus warns the disciples about his coming death, he says that he must "be killed, and on the third day be raised" (Matt 16:21). In saying this, Jesus is alluding to the words of the prophet Hosea. Hosea prophesied to the people of the Northern Kingdom before they were conquered by the Assyrians in 721 BCE. As Hosea called the people to repent, he said:

> Come, let us return to the LORD;
>   for it is he who has torn, and he will heal us;
> he has struck down, and he will bind up.
> After two days he will revive us;
>   on the third day he will raise us up,
>   that we may live before him. (Hos 6:1–2)

Jesus is warning his disciples that he, too, will be struck down, but he will then rise up. He is telling his disciples this so that, when the time comes, at that terrible time, they will not lose faith but will live in hope.

WHAT KIND OF MESSIAH?

After warning the disciples of his coming death, Jesus instructs them that those who want to be his disciples will also have to "take up their cross" (Matt 16:24). Jesus was, of course, not the only person ever to have been crucified. Others, too, endured this most ignominious punishment. He then says something that seems completely incomprehensible, given that he expects to be killed. Jesus says, "For the Son of Man is to come with his angels in the glory of his Father, and then he will repay everyone for what has been done. Truly I tell you, there are some standing here who will not taste death before they see the Son of Man coming in his kingdom" (Matt 16:27–28).

Which is it? Is Jesus, the Son of Man, going to be defeated by his enemies and killed, or is Jesus, the Son of Man, going to come in glory and in power? Are these two ideas in any way compatible? As post-resurrection readers, looking at things in hindsight, Matthew's audience and we realize that both understandings are true, but to Jesus's contemporaries the two concepts were hard to reconcile.

The idea that when the Son of Man comes people will be held accountable for their actions would not be new to Jesus's disciples or Matthew's audience. They already knew and believed what is taught in Psalm 62:

> Once God has spoken;
> twice have I heard this:
> that power belongs to God,
> and steadfast love belongs to you, O Lord.
> For you repay to all
> according to their work. (Ps 62:11–12)

GOD'S GLORY REVEALED

Matthew's account of the transfiguration (Matt 17:1–8) would recall to Jewish readers God's appearance to Moses on Mount Sinai. Matthew tells us that the vision occurred "six days" (Matt 17:1) after Jesus told his disciples that the Son of Man would come in glory (Matt 16:27). Moses waited six days on the mountain before God spoke to him from a cloud (see Exod 24:16). Like Moses, Jesus and three of his disciples were on a high mountain when Jesus was transfigured before them, and when God spoke to them from a cloud.

Peter, James, and John see not only Jesus transfigured, but also Moses and Elijah talking with Jesus. We already know the significance of Moses and Elijah. Moses received the Ten Commandments on Mount Sinai, and Elijah was the prophet who was expected to prepare the way of the Lord. Together they represent the Law and the prophets. Remember, Jesus has already said that he did not come to destroy the Law and the prophets, but to fulfill them (Matt 5:17).

Peter's response to seeing Moses and Elijah with Jesus is to offer to "make three dwellings here, one for you, one for Moses, and one for Elijah" (Matt 17:4). The word *dwelling* is synonymous with the words *tent* and *tabernacle.* God traveled with the Israelites through the desert in a tent/tabernacle/dwelling place for forty years during the exodus. Peter is suggesting that Moses and Elijah (that is, the Law and the prophets), continue to dwell with them, just as Jesus will.

God's voice from heaven says, "This is my Son, the Beloved; with him I am well pleased; listen to him!" (Matt 17:5). As you read this, put the emphasis on *This* and on *him*: "**This** is my Son, the Beloved…; listen to **him**!" When the disciples overcome their fear and look up, only Jesus remains. Matthew is teaching that Jesus, Moses, and Elijah are not three people of equal authority. Only Jesus is God's own Son. The ramification of this teaching is that when the Pharisees, scribes, and Sadducees disagree with Jesus on how to interpret the Law and the prophets, the disciples are to listen to Jesus.

As they come down from the mountain, Jesus once again warns his disciples not to tell anyone about their vision until "after the Son of Man has been raised from the dead" (Matt 17:9). The disciples will understand much more after the resurrection. Jesus also identifies the expected role of Elijah with the role of John the Baptist, as he did before (see Matt 11:14). Jesus says, "Elijah is indeed coming and will restore all things; but I tell you that Elijah has already come, and they did not recognize him, but they did to him whatever they pleased. So also the Son of Man is about to suffer at their hands" (Matt 17:11–12). Matthew then tells us that "the disciples understood that he was speaking to them about John the Baptist" (Matt 17:13).

MATTHEW CONCLUDES HIS FOURTH NARRATIVE SECTION

As Matthew concludes his fourth narrative section about Jesus and introduces Jesus's fourth discourse, he tells the story of Jesus curing a boy who suffers from seizures. The father of the boy tells Jesus that his disciples were unable to cure his son. Hearing this, Jesus laments the lack of faith in his contemporaries. Jesus says, "You faithless and perverse generation, how much longer must I be with you?" (Matt 17:17). Here Jesus echoes the words Moses attributes to God when God laments the people's lack of faith. God says, "they are a perverse generation, children in whom there is no faithfulness" (Deut 32:20b).

Next, Jesus warns his disciples for the second time that the Son of Man is going to be killed and that he will be raised on the third day. The disciples are "greatly distressed" (Matt 17:23), but they do not argue with Jesus this time.

Matthew's last story is a puzzling one. The collectors of the Temple tax ask Peter if Jesus pays the tax. Peter says that he does. We read about the Temple tax in the Book of Exodus: "Each one who is registered, from twenty years old and upward, shall give the Lord's offering. The rich shall not give more, and the poor shall not give less, than the half shekel, when you bring this offering to the Lord to make atonement for your lives" (Exod 30:14–15). Jesus agrees to pay the tax, but he does not agree that he owes it. Why? Because kings don't ask their own children to pay a toll or tribute to them. Jesus is implying that, because he is God's Son, he does not owe the tax. However, he will pay it so as not to "give offense" (Matt 17:27). This story is a perfect introduction to Jesus's fourth discourse, which deals with how to behave so as to heal divisions in community life.

COMMUNITY PROBLEMS

Jesus's fourth discourse, unlike his previous three, does not include many allusions to the Old Testament. In fact, as Jesus teaches his disciples important lessons about community life, there are only three Old Testament allusions that can be cited as background information on how Jesus is fulfilling the Law and the prophets, on how Jesus is challenging his disciples to grow in their understanding of the ramifications of the truth that God is love and is calling God's people to love one another.

Jesus's lessons on loving behavior within a community begin with him answering a question: "Who is the greatest in the kingdom of heaven?" (Matt 18:1). In response, Jesus teaches his disciples not to seek rank, but to imitate a child, realizing that they are God's children, entirely dependent on God, and using their God-given gifts to serve others, not to achieve greatness.

Jesus then warns his disciples always to avoid scandal. To set an example that turns out to be a stumbling block for others is a terrible thing to do. It would be better to drown in the sea than to cause another such harm. If it is your hand, eye, or foot, that causes you to sin, rip it out! This is, of course, irony. It is not your hand, eye, or foot that causes one to sin. It is lack of love in the heart. The teaching calls for internal conversion.

If members of the community—the sheep—go astray, try to win them back. It is God's will that not a single person be lost (Matt 18:14). (We have already discussed the deep Old Testament roots of the sheep/shepherd imagery.)

Jesus continues to build on the teachings in the Jewish Scriptures when instructing his disciples on how to respond when someone sins against them. Jesus teaches the disciples that if someone sins against them, they should first "go and point out the fault when the two of you are alone" (Matt 18:15). The Book of Leviticus teaches the same thing when it pictures God saying, "You shall not hate in your heart anyone of your kin;

you shall reprove your neighbor, or you will incur guilt yourself. You shall not take vengeance or bear a grudge against any of your people, but you shall love your neighbor as yourself: I am the LORD" (Lev 19:17–18).

If speaking to their neighbor privately does not result in reconciliation, the disciples are to bring two or three witnesses and try again to reconcile. This instruction about bringing witnesses is also given in the Book of Deuteronomy: "A single witness shall not suffice to convict a person of any crime or wrongdoing in connection with any offense that may be committed. Only on the evidence of two or three witnesses shall a charge be sustained" (Deut 19:15). However, the intent behind Jesus's teaching is different from that in Deuteronomy in that Jesus's goal is not conviction, but reconciliation.

If the person who caused the offense will not listen to a private correction, the intervention with three witnesses, or the whole church community, only then can the person be excluded from the community. They can then be treated like "a Gentile and a tax collector" (Matt 18:17). This, too, is an ironic statement. Remember how Jesus treated Gentiles (he healed the daughter of the Canaanite woman) and tax collectors (he called a tax collector to be one of his disciples). If the offender had a change of heart and was no longer causing division in the community, Jesus would welcome that person back.

As part of his teaching on how to correct a member of the community, Jesus gives authority to the disciples that he earlier gave to Peter. Jesus says, "Truly I tell you, whatever you bind on earth will be bound in heaven, and whatever you loose on earth will be loosed in heaven" (Matt 18:18; see also Matt 16:19). This teaching, too, is to promote unity. The community can agree on teachings and require that they be obeyed. When the community comes to agreement on such decisions, Christ is "there among them" (Matt 18:20).

Jesus concludes his fourth discourse by once more teaching the absolute necessity of forgiveness. He teaches Peter that he must forgive "seventy-seven times" (Matt 18:22), that is, always. (Remember that the number seven represents fullness, completeness.) The parable of the unforgiving servant reinforces the necessity of forgiveness by reminding the disciples that they are God's servants, sinners who have been forgiven. They must therefore forgive others. Jesus had previously pointed this out when he taught the disciples how to pray, saying, "Forgive us our debts, as we also have forgiven our debtors" (Matt 6:12).

Matthew then tells us, "When Jesus had finished saying these things, he left Galilee and went to the region of Judea" (Matt 19:1). Matthew has set the stage for his fifth narrative about Jesus and discourse by Jesus.

8

THE END TIME IS NEAR! BE PREPARED!

In Matthew's fifth section, which, once more, is composed of a narrative about Jesus (Matt 19:1—23:39) and a discourse by Jesus (Matt 24:1—25:46), Matthew describes the end times of Jesus's public ministry and pictures Jesus warning his disciples to be prepared for the end time when the Son of Man will come in glory.

Even though Jesus has traveled from Galilee to the region of Judea, his controversies with the Pharisees continue. As is his practice, Jesus quotes the Law, the most respected source of authority for the Pharisees, as he answers their questions, questions asked to test Jesus, not to learn from him. This time the Pharisees ask Jesus, "Is it lawful for a man to divorce his wife for any cause?" (Matt 19:3). Jesus, of course, knows that the Pharisees are basing their question on instructions in the Book of Deuteronomy. In these instructions, divorce is not forbidden; it is simply regulated. Deuteronomy says,

> Suppose a man enters into marriage with a woman, but she does not please him because he finds something objectionable about her, and so he writes her a certificate of divorce, puts it in her hand, and sends her out of his house; she then leaves his house and goes off to become another man's wife. Then suppose the second man dislikes her, writes her a bill of divorce, puts it in her hand, and sends her out of his house

> (or the second man who married her dies); her first husband, who sent her away, is not permitted to take her again to be his wife after she has been defiled; for that would be abhorrent to the LORD. (Deut 24:1–4)

Jesus does not at all agree that a man has a right to divorce his wife for any cause, no matter how trivial. Jesus agrees with the fifth-century prophet Malachi, who explained to the returned exiles in Jerusalem that marriage was a covenant relationship that could not be broken. Malachi says, "The LORD was a witness between you and the wife of your youth, to whom you have been faithless, though she is your companion and your wife by covenant. Did not one God make her? Both flesh and spirit are his. And what does the one God desire? Godly offspring. So look to yourselves and do not let anyone be faithless to the wife of his youth. For I hate divorce, says the LORD, the God of Israel" (Mal 2:14–16a).

As Jesus argues with the Pharisees, he quotes Genesis 1:27 and 2:24. Jesus says, "Have you not read that the one who made them at the beginning 'made them male and female' and said, 'For this reason a man shall leave his father and mother and be joined to his wife, and the two shall become one flesh?' So they are no longer two, but one flesh. Therefore what God has joined together, let no one separate" (Matt 19:4–6). The Pharisees counter with the argument from Deuteronomy 24:1, asking, "Why then did Moses command us to give a certificate of dismissal and to divorce her?" (Matt 19:7). Jesus then repeats the teaching he gave previously during the Sermon on the Mount (see Matt 5:31–32). Jesus claims divorce was allowed because of people's hardheartedness. Jesus continues to teach strongly against it, saying, "And I say to you, whoever divorces his wife, except for unchastity, and marries another commits adultery" (Matt 19:9).

Scripture scholars ask why this question about divorce is *testing* Jesus. Surely the Pharisees must realize that Jesus knows the law as well as, or better than, they do. Some suggest that the test was to get Jesus to condemn divorce again now that he is back in Judea, under Herod Antipas's authority. Criticizing Herod's marriage got John the Baptist killed. The Pharisees want Jesus dead too.

The disciples then suggest that, since a man should not divorce his wife, perhaps it would be better not to marry in the first place. Jesus replies that some people are eunuchs from birth, some are castrated for royal duty (that is, to take care of the king's harem; see Esth 1:10; 2:3, 14, 21), and some do not marry "for the sake of the kingdom of heaven" (Matt 19:12). The reward for eunuchs who serve the Lord is described in Isaiah:

> And do not let the eunuch say,
>   "I am just a dry tree."
> For thus says the LORD:
> To the eunuchs who keep my sabbaths,
>   who choose the things that please me
>   and hold fast my covenant,
> I will give, in my house, and within my walls
>   a monument and a name
>   better than sons and daughters;
> I will give them an everlasting name
>   that shall not be cut off. (Isa 56:3b–5)

Next, the disciples try to block people from bringing children to Jesus to receive his blessing. Jesus intervenes, saying, "Let the little children come to me, and do not stop them; for it is to such as these that the kingdom of heaven belongs" (Matt 19:14). Remember that Jesus used a child as an example when the disciples asked who is greatest in the kingdom of heaven (see Matt 18:1–5). Jesus is constantly teaching that the kingdom is not about power and authority; it is about knowing and doing God's will. For the disciples, coming to understand what constitutes *the kingdom* is obviously a slow process.

WHAT GOOD DEED MUST I DO?

The next person to question Jesus is not an adversary but a sincere, young, wealthy man. He asks Jesus, "What good deed must I do to have eternal life?" (Matt 19:16). In answering this question, Jesus quotes the Law, just as he did with the Pharisees. Jesus says, "If you wish to enter into life, keep the commandments" (Matt 19:17). Jesus then repeats the fifth, sixth, seventh, eighth, and fourth commandments as they are taught in the Book of Exodus (see Exod 20:12–16). Jesus says: "You shall not murder; You shall not commit adultery; You shall not steal; You shall not bear false witness; Honor your father and mother" (Matt 19:18–19a). Jesus then adds the teaching from Leviticus 19:18: "You shall love your neighbor as yourself" (Matt 19:19b). The young man is already obeying the commandments. He has a desire to do more. He asks, "What do I still lack?" (Matt 19:20). Jesus then tells the young man what he, personally, could do to fulfill his spiritual longing. He could sell his possessions, give the money to the poor, and become a disciple of Jesus. The man is not yet ready to do that. He goes away sad, still spiritually unfulfilled.

After this exchange, Jesus tells the disciples that it is hard for rich people to enter the kingdom of heaven because they are too attached to their riches. This astounds the disciples. Riches were understood to be a blessing from God, not an obstacle to entering the kingdom. In response to the disciples' question, "Then who can be saved?" Jesus says, "For mortals it is impossible, but for God all things are possible" (Matt 19:26). This insight is one that the author of the Book of Job also offers. After confronting God because of his suffering, Job admits his misunderstandings, saying, "I know that you can do all things, and that no purpose of yours can be thwarted" (Job 42:2).

Drawing a contrast between himself and the rich young man, Peter says, "Look, we have left everything and followed you. What then shall we have?" (Matt 19:27). At this point, Jesus once again alludes to the Book of Daniel in which Daniel has a vision of the heavenly court and of God giving the Son of Man authority over all nations. The Book of Daniel says:

> Thrones were set in place
> and one of great age took his seat.
> His robe was white as snow,
> the hair of his head as pure as wool.
> His throne was a blaze of flames,
> its wheels were a burning fire.
> A stream of fire poured out,

issuing from his presence.
A thousand thousand waited on him,
ten thousand times ten thousand stood before him.
A court was held
and the books were opened....
I gazed into the visions of the night.
And I saw, coming on the clouds of heaven,
one like a son of man.
He came to the one of great age
and was led into his presence.
On him was conferred sovereignty,
glory and kingship,
and men of all peoples, nations and languages became his servants.
His sovereignty is an eternal sovereignty
which shall never pass away,
nor will his empire ever be destroyed. (Dan 7:9–10, 13–14;
Jerusalem Bible translation)

Alluding to this passage, Jesus tells his disciples that "at the renewal of all things, when the Son of Man is seated on the throne of his glory, you who have followed me will also sit on twelve thrones, judging the twelve tribes of Israel" (Matt 19:28).

The disciples should not get all puffed up and proud over the role that they have received and accepted. They have received this role as a gift. Such gifts cannot be earned. That is what Jesus teaches next through the parable of the vineyard workers in response to Peter's question, "Look, we have left everything and followed you. What then will we have?" (Matt 19:27).

In this parable (see Matt 20:1–16), a vineyard owner hires laborers for his vineyard at various times of day. He pays the all-day workers a just, agreed-upon wage. The problem is that he pays everyone the same wage, no matter when they began to work. The all-day workers complain that they have been mistreated. The owner greets the complainers as "friends" and defends himself by saying, "I am doing you no wrong; did you not agree with me for the usual daily wage? Take what belongs to you and go; I choose to give to this last the same as I give to you. Am

I not allowed to do what I choose with what belongs to me? Or are you envious because I am generous?" (Matt 20:13–15).

The disciples, to whom the parable is addressed, can be compared to the workers in the vineyard. All of the workers are there because they were invited. None earned the invitation. All of the workers are treated justly. The problem is that some receive a lot more than they have "earned." The disciples should realize that by following Jesus they are receiving great gifts, not earning rewards. Gratitude, not pride, is the appropriate response.

The Gospel itself does not allegorize this parable and attribute the allegorical interpretation to Jesus. However, the parable, if treated as an allegory, contains a valuable lesson for the Pharisees, too. A vineyard is an established metaphor for God's people, Israel. In Isaiah we read:

> Let me sing for my beloved
> my love-song concerning his vineyard:
> My beloved had a vineyard
> on a very fertile hill.
> He dug it and cleared it of stones,
> and planted it with choice vines;
> he built a watchtower in the midst of it,
> and hewed out a wine vat in it;
> he expected it to yield grapes,
> but it yielded wild grapes.
>
> And now, inhabitants of Jerusalem
> and people of Judah,
> judge between me
> and my vineyard.
> What more was there to do for my vineyard
> that I have not done in it? (Isa 5:1–4a)

The Pharisees who wanted to silence Jesus, all-day workers in their own minds, objected to Jesus reaching out to tax collectors and sinners and inviting them into the kingdom on an equal basis with them. They needed to hear the same lesson that Jesus is teaching the disciples. In any setting—whether addressed to the disciples; to the Pharisees who challenged Jesus; to Matthew's contemporary Jewish/Christian audience who was having to accept the idea that Gentiles, too, were God's chosen people; or to us—the parable cautions us that we, God's people, are not to interpret our gifts as personal accomplishments. We are to accept them with gratitude and not resent that God is generous, not only to us, but to others, too, others who we might think are unworthy.

CAN YOU DRINK MY CUP?

While they are going up to Jerusalem, Jesus, for the third time, warns the disciples that he is going to be killed. Once again referring to himself as "Son of Man," he is specific that the chief priests, scribes, and Gentiles will all play a role in his coming death, a crucifixion. This time we are told nothing about the disciples' reaction.

However, we do hear about the disciples' reaction when the mother of the sons of Zebedee (James and John, but Matthew does not name them) asks that her sons receive special honor, special rank in the kingdom. James and John know what their mother is doing because Jesus asks them, "Are you able to drink the cup that I am about to drink?" (Matt 20:22b). They claim that they are. Jesus tells them that they will indeed drink that cup, but the positions of honor in the kingdom are not his to give. When the other disciples hear this, "they were angry with the two brothers" (Matt 20:24). This gives Jesus the opportunity to teach them once more that the kingdom is not about rank and honor. Those with authority in the kingdom will use that authority to serve, not to rule. They are to model themselves after Jesus. Jesus says that "whoever wishes to be great among you must be your servant, and whoever wishes to be first among you must be your slave, just as the Son of Man came not to be served but to serve, and to give his life as a ransom for many" (Matt 20:26–28). What a mystery this must have been for the disciples. The "Son of Man," who is to come in glory and rule all nations, is to be a servant who is crucified? How can this be true?

As the disciples ponder this deep mystery, Jesus adds authority to the truth of his paradoxical teaching by healing two blind men. The men shout out, "Lord, have mercy on us, Son of David!" (Matt 20:30). "Lord" (the opposite of a servant), "Son of David" (an expected geopolitical king), are words addressed to Jesus, and he responds to them. Jesus asks, "What do you want me to do for you?" (Matt 20:14). Is Jesus, the Son of Man who is going to be killed, who is a servant to all, also "Lord" and "Son of David"? Matthew tells us that he is by picturing Jesus performing yet another mighty sign: "Moved with compassion, Jesus touched their eyes. Immediately they regained their sight and followed him" (Matt 20:34).

JESUS ENTERS JERUSALEM

Matthew's account of Jesus's entrance into Jerusalem includes many Old Testament allusions, including his tenth fulfillment citation. As Jesus nears Jerusalem (also called *Zion,* the cultic and governmental center of Judea), he gives his disciples instructions to go into a nearby village and bring back a donkey and a colt. If they are asked why they are taking the donkey and the colt, they are to say, "The Lord needs them" (Matt 21:3). Notice that Jesus here refers to himself as "Lord." Matthew then says,

> This took place to fulfill what had been spoken through the prophet, saying,
> "Tell the daughter of Zion,
> Look, your king is coming to you,
> humble, and mounted on a donkey,
> and on a colt, the foal of a donkey." (Matt 21:4–5)

Here, Matthew is alluding to the books of Isaiah and Zechariah. In Isaiah we read:

> The LORD has proclaimed
> to the end of the earth:
> Say to daughter Zion,
> "See, your salvation comes;
> his reward is with him,
> and his recompense before him."

They shall be called, "The Holy People,
The Redeemed of the LORD";
and you shall be called, "Sought Out,
A City Not Forsaken." (Isa 62:11–12)

This prophecy was addressed to the inhabitants of Jerusalem who had returned from exile in Babylon and who were rebuilding the city after it had been destroyed by the Babylonians.

Matthew combines this message of hope to "daughter Zion" with a passage from the Book of Zechariah. Zechariah is also encouraging those trying to rebuild Jerusalem, a long and arduous task. The oracles in this section of Zechariah (chapters 9—14) were preached about two hundred years after the Israelites had returned to Jerusalem. The Israelites had been without self-rule, without their own king, for all that time. The prophet is offering the Israelites hope when he says:

Rejoice greatly, O daughter Zion!
Shout aloud, O daughter Jerusalem!
Lo, your king comes to you;
triumphant and victorious is he,
humble and riding on a donkey,
on a colt, the foal of a donkey.
He will cut off the chariot from Ephraim
and the war-horse from Jerusalem:
and the battle bow shall be cut off,
and he shall command peace to the nations;
his dominion shall be from sea to sea,
and from the River to the ends of the earth. (Zech 9:9–10)

The king whom Zechariah pictures is not a mighty conqueror on a splendid horse, armed with a bow. This king will not bring war, but peace. He will be a humble person, not a dictator. God has promised, and the people should continue to have faith that God will be faithful to God's promises.

As Jesus enters Jerusalem, an enormous crowd greets him, shouting, "Hosanna to the Son of David! / Blessed is the one who comes in the name of the Lord! / Hosanna in the highest heaven!" (Matt 21:9). The word *hosanna* is a Hebrew word that means *please save us*. In addition to addressing Jesus as "Son of David," the people who welcome and praise Jesus are quoting Psalm 118, a psalm of victory, giving thanks to the Lord for saving God's people. The psalmist says:

> Save us, we beseech you, O LORD!
> O LORD, we beseech you, give us success!
> Blessed is the one who comes in the name of the LORD.
> We bless you from the house of the LORD. (Ps 118:25–26)

As Matthew describes Jesus entering Jerusalem, he once more centers the readers' attention on Jesus's identity. The people ask, "Who is this?" (Matt 21:10). Those who respond have not begun to understand the whole truth. They answer, "This is the prophet Jesus from Nazareth in Galilee" (Matt 21:11).

CONFRONTATIONS GROW

As Jesus enters the Temple, he sees that people are there, not to pray, but to buy and sell. Jesus accuses the merchants, saying, "It is written, 'My house shall be called a house of prayer'; but you are making it a den of robbers" (Matt 21:13). Here Jesus is quoting both Isaiah and Jeremiah.

In Isaiah 56, the author is teaching that God will include non-Israelites in God's saving actions. Isaiah pictures the Lord saying:

> And the foreigners who join themselves to the LORD,
> to minister to him, to love the name of the LORD,
> and to be his servants,
> all who keep the sabbath, and do not profane it,
> and hold fast my covenant—
> these I will bring to my holy mountain,
> and make them joyful in my house of prayer;
> their burnt offerings and their sacrifices
> will be accepted on my altar;

for my house shall be called a house of prayer
for all peoples. (Isa 56:6–7)

Jesus combines this last line from Isaiah with a quotation from Jeremiah. Jeremiah is challenging those who disobey the Ten Commandments and then come to pray in the Temple. Jeremiah pictures God saying: "Will you steal, murder, commit adultery, swear falsely, make offerings to Baal, and go after other gods that you have not known, and then come and stand before me in this house, which is called by my name, and say, 'We are safe!'—only to go on doing all these abominations? Has this house, which is called by my name, become a den of robbers in your sight? You know, I too am watching, says the LORD" (Jer 7:9–11). Jesus shares Jeremiah's outrage that some people are not treating the Temple as a place of prayer.

Jesus continues to perform mighty signs, curing the blind and the lame. The chief priests and scribes are alarmed both by Jesus's power and by the fact that the people are still calling out, "Hosanna to the Son of David" (Matt 21:15). His adversaries give Jesus the opportunity to deny that he deserves such a title, saying, "Do you hear what these are saying?" (Matt 21:16). As Jesus responds, he once more quotes a psalm. Jesus says: "Yes; have you never read, 'Out of the mouths of infants and nursing babies / you have prepared praise for yourself'?" (Matt 21:16). Here Jesus is alluding to Psalm 8, which begins:

Yahweh, our Lord,
how great your name throughout the earth!
Above the heavens is your majesty chanted
by the mouths of children, babes in arms. (Ps 8:1–2; Jerusalem Bible translation)

In quoting this hymn that praises God for the magnificence of all of creation, including human beings, Jesus is accepting, not denying, the people's claims about him. Jesus is the Son of David, and he has come to save. "Hosanna to the Son of David!" Out of the mouths of babes and children (the crowd, not the highly educated chief priests and scribes) the truth is being proclaimed.

The next time Matthew describes Jesus as quoting the Old Testament is when Jesus tells the parable of the wicked tenants in the vineyard to the chief priests and Pharisees. Between this parable and the story of Jesus's cleansing of the Temple, Matthew continues to depict Jesus's growing frustration as well as the Pharisees' and scribes' growing opposition to him. After leaving Jerusalem and then returning the next morning, Jesus curses the fig tree for not bearing fruit. This episode becomes a lesson on the power of faith (Matt 21:18–22). Jesus then, once more, enters the Temple and is confronted by the Pharisees, who question the source of his authority. In response, Jesus tells them three parables of judgment: the parable of the two sons (Matt 21:18–32), the parable of the wicked tenants (Matt 21:33–41), and the parable of the wedding feast (Matt 22:1–14). It is while telling the parable of the wicked tenants that Jesus once more quotes Scripture.

In the parable, a landowner who has a vineyard leases it to tenants. When it is time for the harvest, the landlord sends his slaves to the tenants to collect his crops. The tenants "beat one, killed another, and stoned another" (Matt 21:35). The landowner then decides to send his son, expecting the tenants to treat him with respect. The tenants kill his son too. Jesus then asks the Pharisees and the chief priests, "Now when the owner of the vineyard comes, what will he do to those tenants?" (Matt 21:40). The Pharisees and chief priests respond with a harsh judgment, a judgment that they do not yet realize they are passing on themselves: "He will put those wretches to a miserable death, and lease the vineyard to other tenants who will give him the produce at the harvest time" (Matt 21:41).

Jesus then challenges his adversaries, saying,

> Have you never read in the scriptures:
> "The stone that the builders rejected
> has become the cornerstone;
> this was the Lord's doing,
> and it is amazing in our eyes"? (Matt 21:42)

Here, Jesus is quoting Psalm 118 and is referring to himself as the cornerstone. He accuses the chief priests and Pharisees of being the builders who reject him.

Psalm 118 is a song of victory. The speaker is giving thanks to God for saving him. The psalmist says:

> I thank you that you have answered me
>   and have become my salvation.
> The stone that the builders rejected
>   has become the chief cornerstone.
> This is the LORD's doing;
>   it is marvelous in our eyes. (Ps 118:21–23)

The psalmist is claiming that a person, perhaps himself, was considered a loser but has now become victorious and central to God's plans. He gives all the credit to God.

In quoting this passage, Jesus warns the Pharisees and chief priests that by rejecting him they are failing God's people (we have already mentioned the vineyard as a metaphor for God's people; see Isa 5:1–7). Jesus tells them this directly when he says, "Therefore I tell you, the kingdom of God will be taken away from you and given to a people that produces the fruits of the kingdom" (Matt 21:43). The Pharisees understand exactly what Jesus is saying, and they want to arrest him all the more.

We know that the early Church used this passage from Psalm 118 that Jesus quotes in Matthew to come to terms with Jesus's rejection by the leaders of his own people. For instance, in Acts we read that when Peter and John were preaching about Jesus's resurrection, Peter healed a crippled man who was being carried into the Temple. Peter and John were arrested by the priests and Sadducees. In his own defense, Peter said, "Rulers of the people and elders, if we are questioned today because of a good deed done to someone who was sick and are asked how this man has been healed, let it be known to all of you, and to all the people of Israel, that this man is standing before you in good health by the name of Jesus Christ of Nazareth, whom you crucified, whom God raised from the dead. This Jesus is 'the stone that was rejected by you, the builders; it has become the cornerstone.' There is salvation in no one else, for there is no other name under heaven given among mortals by which we must be saved" (Acts 4:8b–12).

Matthew's next two accounts do not include Old Testament quotations. The parable of the wedding banquet (Matt 22:1–14) teaches that all are invited to the kingdom, but not all accept the invitation (that is, Jesus's adversaries). The question about paying taxes (Matt 22:15–22) reveals the hypocrisy of Jesus's questioners who want to trap Jesus by having him antagonize either the Pharisees, who object to paying taxes to Roman rulers, or the Herodians, who cooperate with the civil government. Jesus avoids the trap. It is not until Jesus is confronted by the Sadducees (Matt 22:23–33), who deny life after death, that Jesus once more quotes Scripture.

The Sadducees, too, are not trying to learn from Jesus but are trying to challenge his teachings. They pose a question that they think Jesus will not be able to answer to their satisfaction. The Sadducees did not accept as authoritative all of what had become Jewish Scripture. In Jesus's time, there were three sections to the Jewish Scriptures: the Law, the Prophets, and the Writings. The Sadducees accepted only the Law (the first five books, called the Pentateuch; also called the Torah). So, they refer to the Book of Deuteronomy when they say, "Moses said, 'If a man dies childless, his brother shall marry the widow, and raise up children for his brother'" (Matt 22:24). The Sadducees are correctly alluding to the Book of Deuteronomy. Deuteronomy says: "When brothers reside together, and one of them dies and has no son, the wife of the deceased shall not be married outside the family to a stranger. Her husband's brother shall go in to her, taking her in marriage, and performing the duty of a husband's brother to her, and the firstborn whom she bears shall succeed to the name of the deceased brother, so that his name may not be blotted out of Israel" (Deut 25:5–6). Their question is, if seven brothers all marry the same wife, whose wife will she be in the resurrection?

As mentioned in our last chapter, the Israelites gradually came to a belief in life after death. We quoted a passage from Wisdom that supports a belief in life after death. Another book, written in the second century BCE, the Book of Daniel, also supports the idea of life after death. In describing the time of the end, the Book of Daniel says: "Many of those who sleep in the dust of the earth shall awake, some to everlasting life, and some to shame and everlasting contempt. Those who are wise shall shine like the brightness of the sky, and those who lead many to righteousness, like the stars forever and ever" (Dan 12:2–3).

Unlike the Sadducees, Jesus accepts all three sections of the Jewish Scriptures as authoritative. We know this because Matthew has pictured Jesus quoting all five books from the Law (Genesis, Exodus, Leviticus, Numbers, Deuteronomy), seven books from the section called the Prophets (Samuel, Kings, Isaiah, Ezekiel, Hosea, Jonah, Malachi), and three books from the section called the Writings (Psalms, Jonah, Daniel; while Daniel is listed among the Prophets in the Christian Bible, this book is among the Writings in the Jewish Scriptures). So, Jesus could have quoted Daniel to support his belief in life after death. After all, he quotes Daniel regularly as he refers to himself as the "Son of Man" and tells the disciples that the Son of Man will come in the "glory of his Father and then he will repay everyone for what has been done" (Matt 16:27; see Dan 7:13–14).

However, Jesus knows perfectly well that the Sadducees would not be persuaded by words from the Book of Daniel since it is not part of the Pentateuch. So, Jesus quotes the Book of Exodus. First Jesus accuses the Sadducees of not knowing "the scriptures nor the power of God" (Matt 22:29). He then says, "For in the resurrection they neither marry nor are given in marriage, but are like angels in heaven. And as for the resurrection of the dead, have you not read what was said to you by God, 'I am the God of Abraham, the God of Isaac, and the God of Jacob'? He is God not of the dead, but of the living" (Matt 22:31–32). Here, Jesus is quoting God's words to Moses at the burning bush. God says, "I am the God of your father, the God of Abraham, the God of Isaac, and the God of Jacob" (Exod 3:6). Based on Scripture and reason, Jesus supports the belief in life after death. The Sadducees have nothing to say in reply.

The Pharisees are the next to try to test Jesus. A lawyer asks Jesus which commandment in the Law is the greatest. Jesus responds, "'You shall love the Lord your God with all your heart, and with all your soul, and with all your mind.' This is the greatest and first commandment. And a second is like it: 'You shall love your neighbor as yourself'" (Matt 22:37–39). With this answer Jesus is quoting both Deuteronomy and Leviticus. In Deuteronomy, Moses teaches the people, saying: "Hear O Israel: The LORD is our God, the LORD alone. You shall love the LORD your God with all your heart, and with all your soul, and with all your might. Keep these words that I am commanding you today in your heart" (Deut 6:4–6). In Leviticus, the Lord instructs Moses to teach the people: "You shall not take vengeance or bear a grudge against any of your people, but you shall love your neighbor as yourself: I am the LORD" (Lev 19:18). Jesus previously quoted this passage when he was speaking to the rich young man (Matt 19:19). Jesus then adds, "On these two commandments hang all the law and the prophets" (Matt 22:40). The Pharisees can't object to a word Jesus is saying. Jesus is a faithful Jew who, unlike the Sadducees, accepts both the Law and the prophets. Jesus is immersed in Scripture and quotes it constantly and accurately. Scripture is just as authoritative for Jesus as is it for the Pharisees. Once more, their attempt to trap Jesus is unsuccessful.

Having once more responded to the challenging and argumentative questions posed to him by the Pharisees, each time quoting Scripture, Jesus turns the tables and asks them a question: "'What do you think of the Messiah? Whose son is he?' They said to him, 'The son of David'" (Matt 22:42–43). In asking this question, Jesus is trying to invite and challenge the Pharisees to be open to a new understanding of the kind of messiah that God is sending. We already know that Jesus identifies with the title *son of David*. Those seeking his healing have often called out, "son of David." Certainly, Matthew agrees that Jesus is the son of David. He has been insisting on that truth since the first sentence of his Gospel. So, Jesus's challenging question to the Pharisees is not denying the truth of their statement but is intended to expand their understanding of the Messiah.

Jesus asks,

> How is it then that David by the Spirit calls him Lord, saying,
> "The Lord said to my Lord,
> Sit at my right hand,
> until I put your enemies under your feet"?
> If David thus calls him Lord, how can he be his son?" (Matt 22:43–45)

Here Jesus quotes Psalm 110. This is a royal psalm that was attributed to David. In it, God promises victory to a Davidic king. The psalm begins:

> The LORD says to my Lord,
> "Sit at my right hand
> Until I make your enemies your footstool." (Ps 110:1)

Jesus, too, attributes the speaking voice in the psalm to David. Jesus is claiming that David was inspired by the Spirit to refer to a king in the Davidic line as *my Lord*: "The LORD said to **my Lord**." Therefore, the Lord God must have inspired David to realize that the expected messiah of the Davidic line would be greater than David himself. Otherwise, why would he refer to him as *Lord*? Jesus is challenging the Pharisees to rethink their understanding of both the expected messiah and the expected kingdom. Once more, Jesus's adversaries have no answer. They are silenced.

We know from the Acts of the Apostles that the early Church used this same passage from Psalm 110 to convince their fellow Israelites that Jesus, who rose from the dead, was, and is, the promised and expected Messiah. In Acts, Peter says:

> For David did not ascend into the heavens, but he himself says,
> "The Lord said to my Lord,
> Sit at my right hand,
> until I make your enemies your footstool."
> Therefore, let the entire house of Israel know with certainty that God has made him both Lord and Messiah, this Jesus whom you crucified. (Acts 2:34–36)

WOE TO THE SCRIBES AND PHARISEES

Now that Jesus's controversies with the scribes and Pharisees are over, Jesus warns the crowd and his disciples against these well-educated but closed-minded religious leaders. In doing so, Jesus once more depends on his listeners' knowledge of the Jewish Scripture to understand what he is saying. First, Jesus expresses his respect for religious authority in general when he says, "The scribes and Pharisees sit on Moses' seat; therefore, do whatever they teach you and follow it" (Matt 23:2–3). The problem is not with Jewish Scripture or Jewish traditions. The problem is that the scribes and Pharisees who challenge Jesus value external things—titles, appearances, honor—not internal things—integrity, honesty, love of neighbor.

As an example of showy, exterior behavior, Jesus accuses the Pharisees of broadening their phylacteries (Matt 23:5). Phylacteries were little boxes that contained written laws that the Pharisees wore on their foreheads. They did this in response to a very literal understanding of instructions that Moses gives in Deuteronomy: "Keep these words that I am commanding you today in your heart. Recite them to your children and talk about them when you are at home and when you are away, when you lie down and when you rise. Bind them as a sign on your hand, fix them as an emblem on your forehead, and write them on the doorposts of your house and on your gates" (Deut 6:6–9). To broaden phylacteries is simply to draw others' attention to how pious you want them to think you are. It is not to think always in terms of loving God with all your heart, soul, and might (Deut 6:5) and to have your actions flow from that love.

Jesus also says that the Pharisees make their "fringes long" (Matt 23:5). The instruction to wear fringes on their garments appears in the Book of Numbers:

> The LORD said to Moses: Speak to the Israelites, and tell them to make fringes on the corners of their garments throughout their generations and to put a blue cord on the fringe at each corner. You have the fringe so that, when you see it, you will remember all the commandments of the LORD and do them, and not follow the lust of your own heart and your own eyes. So you shall remember and do all my commandments, and you shall be holy to your God. (Num 15:37–40)

Jesus is not teaching his followers to disobey this law. Jesus obeyed it himself. Remember that Matthew told us earlier that when the woman with the hemorrhages wanted to be healed, she came up behind Jesus "and touched the fringe of his cloak, for she said to herself, 'If I only touch his cloak, I will be made well'" (Matt 9:20–21). To lengthen the fringe is to draw attention to oneself, not to remember and live out the commandments. Jesus is enjoining religious leaders to be humble, not ostentatious. They should be servants, not seeking to be considered superior to others.

Jesus continues to denounce the behavior of the scribes and Pharisees with seven *woes.* A woe is the opposite of a beatitude. In a woe, both a person's bad behavior and the inevitable consequence of that behavior are named. In the process of instructing the disciples and the crowd not to imitate the behavior of the scribes and Pharisees, Jesus makes two allusions to the Jewish Scriptures. Jesus says, "Therefore I send you prophets, sages, and scribes, some of whom you will kill and crucify, and some you will flog in your synagogues and pursue from town to town, so that upon you may come all the righteous blood shed on earth, from the blood of righteous Abel to the blood of Zechariah son of Barachiah, whom you murdered between the sanctuary and the altar" (Matt 23:34–35).

We read about the murder of Abel in the Book of Genesis. Cain, the son of Adam and Eve, is angry at his brother Abel. "Cain rose up against his brother Abel, and killed him. Then the Lord said to Cain, 'Where is your brother Abel?' He said, 'I do not know; am I my brother's keeper?' And the Lord said, 'What have you done? Listen: your brother's blood is crying out to me from the ground'" (Gen 4:8b–10).

Scripture scholars debate to which Zechariah Jesus is referring. The Zechariah after whom one of the prophetic books is named is not known to have been murdered. However, a Zechariah named in 2 Chronicles is killed, although his father is not named Barachiah. Second Chronicles tells us: "Then the spirit of God took possession of Zechariah son of the priest Jehoiada; he stood above the people and said to them, 'Thus says God: Why do you transgress the commandments of the Lord, so that you cannot prosper? Because you have forsaken the Lord, he has also forsaken you.' But they conspired against him, and by command of the king they stoned him to death in the court of the house of the Lord" (2 Chron 24:20–21; the king was Joash, king of Judah 835–796 BCE). Despite the difference in the father's name, the Zechariah named in 2 Chronicles is probably the prophet to whom Jesus is referring. We know from references such as *Father Abraham* and *son of David* that the father-son language is used to describe ancestors and descendants through the generations, not just immediate descendants.

In referring to Abel and Zechariah, Jesus warns the crowds and the disciples that innocent blood has been shed in the past, and innocent blood will be shed in their generation too. Jesus says, "Truly I tell you, all this will come upon this generation" (Matt 23:36).

Jesus's final words before he leaves the Temple are his lament over Jerusalem. Jesus says, "Jerusalem, Jerusalem, the city that kills the prophets and stones those who are sent to it! How often have I desired to gather your children together as a hen gathers her brood under her wings, and you were not willing! See, your house is left to you, desolate. For I tell you, you will not see me again until you say, 'Blessed is the one who comes in the name of the Lord'" (Matt 23:37–39). In this lament, Jesus alludes to the Jewish Scriptures three times.

When Jesus says that he longs to protect the people as a hen protects her brood, Jesus is using the same imagery found in Psalm 36 to express God's profound love for God's people. The psalmist says:

> How precious is your steadfast love, O God!
> All people may take refuge in the shadow of your wings.
> They feast on the abundance of your house,
> and you give them drink from the river of your delights.
> For with you is the fountain of life;
> in your light we see light.
> O continue your steadfast love to those who know you,
> and your salvation to the upright of heart! (Ps 36:7–10)

Jesus continues his steadfast love for God's people, even in the face of rejection.

When Jesus warns, "See, your house is left to you, desolate," he is quoting the prophet Jeremiah, who gave his contemporaries the same warning. Jeremiah is pleading with the people to listen to their God. Jeremiah says:

> Thus says the LORD: Act with justice and righteousness, and deliver from the hand of the oppressor anyone who has been robbed. And do no wrong or violence to the alien, the orphan, and the widow, or shed innocent blood in this place.... But if you will not heed these words, I swear by myself, says the LORD, that this house shall become a desolation. (Jer 22:3, 5)

Jesus's warning as he leaves the Temple that the house, the Temple, would be left desolate would have been difficult for Matthew's contemporary audience to read because the Temple was destroyed in 70 CE, just ten years before Matthew is thought to have written his Gospel.

Finally, when Jesus says that the people will not see him again until they say, "Blessed is the one who comes in the name of the Lord" (Matt 23:39), Jesus is quoting Psalm 118:26, the psalm that Matthew previously quoted when he described the crowds greeting Jesus as he entered Jerusalem (see Matt 21:9). When Jesus says that the people will not see him, he is referring to the fact that he will be put to death. His blood, like the blood of previous martyrs, will be spilled. However, the people will see him again, and when they do, they will recognize that Jesus has come in the name of the Lord.

JESUS'S ESCHATOLOGICAL DISCOURSE

As Jesus leaves the Temple area, he once more warns his disciples that the Temple will be destroyed. He then goes to the Mount of Olives, where he delivers his discourse on the end time (see Matt 24:3—25:46). The very setting of this discourse is an allusion to the Jewish Scripture. In the Book of Zechariah, as the prophet warns his contemporaries (the descendants of the returned exiles who had been without self-rule for several hundred years) about the end times, he describes the Lord arriving on the Mount of Olives to save the people. The prophet says:

> See, a day is coming for the LORD, when the plunder taken from you will be divided in your midst. For I will gather all

> the nations against Jerusalem to battle, and the city shall be taken and the houses looted and the women raped; half the city shall go into exile, but the rest of the people shall not be cut off from the city. Then the LORD will go forth and fight against those nations as when he fights on a day of battle. On that day his feet shall stand on the Mount of Olives which lies before Jerusalem on the east; and the Mount of Olives shall be split in two from east to west by a very wide valley, so that one half of the Mount shall withdraw northward, and the other half southward. And you shall flee by the valley of the LORD's mountain, for the valley between the mountains shall reach to Azal; and you shall flee as you fled from the earthquake in the days of King Uzziah of Judah. Then the LORD my God will come, and all the holy ones with him. (Zech 14:1–5)

While on the Mount of Olives, the disciples ask Jesus: "When will this be, and what will be the sign of your coming and of the end of the age?" (Matt 24:3b). Jesus's response to these questions is filled with Old Testament quotations from all three sections of the Jewish Scriptures: the Law, the Prophets, and the Writings. After warning the disciples that there will be false messiahs, wars, famines, earthquakes, persecutions, and false prophets, he says that these are preliminary signs. Before the end time comes, the good news of the kingdom will be preached to the whole world. He then says, "So when you see the desolating sacrilege standing in the holy place, as was spoken of by the prophet Daniel (let the reader understand), then those in Judea must flee to the mountains" (Matt 24:15–16). The "desolating sacrilege" to which Jesus refers, and which is spoken of in the Book of Daniel, took place in 167 BCE. The king of Syria at that time was Antiochus IV, who persecuted those in Palestine who resisted Hellenistic culture and religion. He invaded Jerusalem and brought about the *abomination of desolation*: he honored the Greek god Zeus in the Temple and had pigs sacrificed on the Temple altar. The Book of Daniel says: "Forces sent by him shall occupy and profane the temple and fortress. They shall abolish the regular burnt offering and set up the abomination that makes desolate. He shall seduce with intrigue those who violate the covenant; but the people who are loyal to their God shall stand firm and take action" (Dan 11:31–32; see also Dan 9:27; 12:11).

Jesus's next allusion to the Old Testament comes when he warns people not to turn back once they are fleeing. Jesus says, "Then those in Judea must flee to the mountains, the one on the housetop must not go down to take what is in the house; the one in the field must not turn back to get a coat" (Matt 24:16–18). This warning is an allusion to the Book of Genesis in which we read the story of Lot's family fleeing Sodom and Gomorrah before they were destroyed. Lot's family was saved because God was being faithful to God's covenant with Abraham, who was Lot's brother. Lot is urged, "Flee for your life; do not look back or stop anywhere in the Plain; flee to the hills, or else you will be consumed.…Then the LORD rained on Sodom and Gomorrah sulfur and fire from the LORD out of heaven; and he overthrew those cities, and all the Plain, and all the inhabitants of the cities, and what grew on the ground. But Lot's wife, behind him, looked back, and she became a pillar of salt" (Gen 19:17, 24–26). This famous story has been used since Old Testament times to teach the importance of perseverance. Jesus teaches the same lesson about not looking back, although in a different setting, in Luke's Gospel when he says, "No one who puts a hand to the plow and looks back is fit for the kingdom of God" (Luke 9:62).

After warning the disciples not to fall for false prophets, Jesus tells them that the coming of the Son of Man will be obvious to all, just as lightning from east to west is obvious to all. He then says, "Where the corpse is, there the vultures will gather" (Matt 24:28). This may be a strange comparison for people who have never seen vultures gather, but it would have been familiar to the original audience. A vulture is a large bird that eats the corpses of dead animals. Here Jesus uses the same imagery as does the author of the Book of Job to describe something that should be easily observed by everyone.

In the Book of Job, written in the sixth century BCE, Job and his so-called friends have a debate about whether an innocent person could suffer. Job thinks the answer is yes because he is suffering, and he has not done anything that would deserve such suffering. He disagrees that his suffering is a punishment for sin. His friends think Job must have sinned and so deserves his suffering. Otherwise, God is neither all powerful nor all loving. After Job challenges God, God appears to Job and challenges him. God agrees with Job's side of the debate; not all suffering is punishment for sin. However, God points out that there are many, many things that Job does not understand, not just why an innocent person might suffer. Job, after all, is neither the center of the universe nor in charge of the universe. As part of his challenge to Job, God says,

> Is it at your command that the eagle mounts up
> and makes its nest on high?
> It lives on the rock and makes its home
> in the fastness of the rocky crag.
> From there it spies the prey;
> its eyes see it from far away.
> Its young ones suck up blood;
> and where the slain are, there it is. (Job 39:27–30)

An eagle, like a vulture, is a bird that eats dead flesh. Jesus and the author of Job use the same example to point out something beyond human understanding but something—the coming of the Son of Man—that will be just as obvious to all as is the presence of a corpse when the vultures gather.

Jesus then further describes the coming of the Son of Man. Jesus says,

> Immediately after the suffering of those days the sun will be darkened, and the moon will not give its light; the stars will fall from heaven, and the powers of heaven will be shaken. Then the sign of the Son of Man will appear in heaven, and then all the tribes of the earth will mourn, and they will see the Son of Man coming on the clouds of heaven with power and great glory. And he will send out his angels with a loud trumpet call, and they will gather his elect from the four winds, from one end of heaven to the other. (Matt 24:29–31)

Nearly all the images in this description are images with which Jesus was familiar because of his immersion in Jewish Scripture.

For instance, when Isaiah describes the punishment Babylon will receive, he uses the same apocalyptic imagery.

> For the stars of the heavens and their constellations
>   will not give their light;
> the sun will be dark at its rising,
>   and the moon will not shed its light. (Isa 13:10)

When Ezekiel prophesies against the Pharaoh in Egypt, he pictures the Lord saying:

> When I blot you out, I will cover the heavens,
>   and make their stars dark;
> I will cover the sun with a cloud,
>   And the moon shall not give its light. (Ezek 32:7)

Jesus's prediction that the tribes of the earth will mourn is reminiscent of the description of the mourning in Jerusalem that we read in the Book of Zechariah:

> And I will pour out a spirit of compassion and supplication on the house of David and the inhabitants of Jerusalem, so that, when they look on the one whom they have pierced, they shall mourn for him, as one mourns for an only child, and weep bitterly over him, as one weeps over a firstborn. (Zech 12:10)

The prophecy of Zechariah says that the house of David and Jerusalem will have a change of heart and will mourn over one whom they have pierced. Who, contemporary with the prophecy, has been pierced? This is a question that Scripture scholars have not been able to answer with certainty. Of course, in hindsight the early Church saw this prophecy fulfilled in Jesus. In John's Gospel, after Jesus's side is pierced, John says, "And again another passage of scripture says, 'They will look on the one whom they have pierced'" (John 19:37).

As we have mentioned many times, Jesus is alluding to the Book of Daniel when he pictures the Son of Man coming on the clouds of heaven:

I gazed into the visions of the night.
And I saw, coming on the clouds of heaven,
one like a son of man....
On him was conferred sovereignty,
glory and kingship,
and men of all peoples, nations, and languages became his servants.
His sovereignty is an eternal sovereignty
which shall never pass away,
nor will his empire ever be destroyed. (Dan 7:13–14; Jerusalem Bible translation)

In the Book of Isaiah, the day on which the Lord delivers the Israelites is announced with a trumpet blast: Isaiah says, "On that day a great trumpet will be blown, and those who are lost in the land of Assyria and those who were driven out to the land of Egypt will come and worship the LORD on the holy mountain at Jerusalem" (Isa 27:13).

Zechariah describes people having been spread abroad like the four winds: "Up, up! Flee from the land of the north, says the LORD; for I have spread you abroad like the four winds of heaven, says the LORD" (Zech 2:6). When the Son of Man comes, the people will be gathered back from the four winds.

As Jesus teaches the disciples that the time of the coming of the Son of Man is imminent, but he does not know exactly when that time will be, for only the Father knows (Matt 24:36), he says, "Heaven and earth will pass away, but my words will not pass away" (Matt 24:35). Here, Jesus alludes to the Book of Isaiah and makes a startling claim about his own identity. Isaiah says, "The grass withers, the flower fades; / but the word of our God will stand forever" (Isa 40:8). Like God's word, Jesus's words will stand forever.

Since no one knows when the Son of Man will come, the people should always be ready. To teach this lesson, Jesus compares the present generation to Noah's generation: "For as the days of Noah were, so will be the coming of the Son of Man. For as in those days before the flood they were eating and drinking, marrying, and giving in marriage, until the day Noah entered the ark, and they knew nothing until the flood came and swept them all away, so too will be the coming of the Son of

Man" (Matt 24:37–39). This is, of course, an allusion to the Book of Genesis in which we read the story of Noah and the flood (see Gen 6:1—9:28).

Jesus continues to teach the importance of always being ready for the coming of the Son of Man and the final judgment by telling three parables: the faithful and unfaithful servants (Matt 24:45–51), the ten bridesmaids (Matt 25:1–13), and the talents (Matt 25:14–30). He then concludes his eschatological discourse by describing the judgment of people of all nations (Matt 25:31–46). Jesus is once more emphasizing what he has constantly claimed, that loving God and loving one's neighbor are inseparable. Even those who don't recognize that by loving and providing for those in need they are loving God will be rewarded. Love of God and love of neighbor fulfill the Law and the prophets.

9

JESUS'S PASSOVER THROUGH DEATH TO RESURRECTION

Chapter 26 of Matthew's Gospel begins: "When Jesus had finished saying all these things, he said to his disciples, 'You know that after two days the Passover is coming, and the Son of Man will be handed over to be crucified'" (Matt 26:1–2). Jesus has finished his fifth and final discourse, and Matthew is now beginning to tell the story of Jesus's passion, death, and resurrection. The chief priests and elders conspire to arrest Jesus and kill him. However, they decide not to do this "during the festival, or there may be a riot among the people" (Matt 26:5). Matthew makes it clear that the Passover celebration is the setting for all that is to happen.

In order to understand all that Matthew will describe, we need to know a little about the Passover celebration, its history, and the way in which it was celebrated during Jesus's lifetime. This background information will make Jesus's behavior and his words more meaningful to readers who, unlike Jesus, Matthew, and their audiences, may not know Jewish customs.

The word *Passover* is used to name the remembrance and celebration of God saving the Israelites from slavery in Egypt. Before the Israelites were able to escape from Egypt, Egypt suffered many plagues. The final plague killed the firstborn of the Egyptians, but the firstborn of the Israelites were spared. The Book of Exodus tells the story: God instructed Moses and Aaron to have the Israelites slaughter an unblemished lamb. Afterward, the Israelites were instructed to do the following.

> Take some of the blood and put it on the two doorposts and the lintel of the houses in which they eat it. They shall eat the lamb that same night; they shall eat it roasted over the fire with unleavened bread and bitter herbs....This is how you shall eat it; your loins girded, your sandals on your feet, and your staff in your hand; and you shall eat it hurriedly. It is the Passover of the LORD. For I will pass through the land of Egypt that night, and I will strike down every firstborn in the land of Egypt, both human beings and animals; on all the gods of Egypt I will execute judgments; I am the LORD. The blood shall be a sign for you on the houses where you live: when I see the blood, I will pass over you, and no plague shall destroy you when I strike the land of Egypt. (Exod 12:7–8, 11–13)

By the time of Jesus, the Israelites had celebrated God's passing over their houses during the last plague for more than one thousand years. However, the celebration had changed, becoming a pilgrim feast that was combined with the Feast of Unleavened Bread. All Jewish males were to travel to Jerusalem for the celebration. The lambs were sacrificed in the Temple, no longer in individual homes, and ten to twenty men would gather in individual homes to eat the Passover meal. The combined celebration lasted for seven days.

Matthew begins his account of the passion, death, and resurrection by having Jesus tell his disciples for a fourth time that he will be killed. This occurs when his disciples complain that a woman who anoints Jesus's head with costly ointment was wasting money. Jesus says that the woman was preparing his body for burial (see Matt 26:6–13).

Judas then goes to the chief priests who are planning to kill Jesus and asks what they will pay him to betray Jesus. They pay him thirty pieces of silver. Judas will later regret his actions, saying, "I have sinned by betraying innocent blood" (Matt 27:4). He will then throw the thirty pieces of silver into the Temple and hang himself (see Matt 27:5). This account is an allusion to two Old Testament passages.

The first allusion is to the Book of Exodus. In Exodus, the people are instructed that if an "ox gores a male or female slave, the owner shall pay to the slave owner thirty shekels of silver, and the ox shall be stoned" (Exod 21:32). (A shekel is a unit of weight, about half an ounce.) Judas has accepted as payment for Jesus's innocent life what a slave owner would be paid for the accidental death of one of his slaves. In the slave owner's case, the coins were for restitution. In Judas's case, they were for betrayal. How could he have done this? Judas cannot bear the guilt.

The second allusion is to the Book of Zechariah. The prophet says that he was instructed by God to become the shepherd of the flock. The prophet obeys and is hired by the sheep merchants. He cares for the flock but is detested by the other shepherds. As time goes on, the shepherd (prophet) is rejected and leaves. As he is leaving, the shepherd says to the sheep merchants, "'If it seems right to you, give me my wages; but if not, keep them.' So they weighed out as my wages thirty shekels of silver. Then the LORD said to me, 'Throw it into the treasury'—this lordly price at which I was valued by them. So I took the thirty shekels of silver and threw them into the treasury in the house of the LORD" (Zech 11:12–13). The phrase "this lordly price at which I was valued by them," is, of course, ironic. The shepherd (God's prophet) has been mistreated and greatly undervalued. He has obeyed God's instructions, has tried to feed God's people, but has been rejected by everyone, the sheep merchants (buyers and sellers of sheep; not shepherds) and the other shepherds (religious leaders of the time). The prophet believes that in rejecting God's prophet they have rejected God. The prophet is not like Judas, who has betrayed his Lord. Rather, he is like Jesus; he has been rejected.

Matthew next describes Jesus celebrating the Passover meal with his disciples, a meal that took place on the first day of the seven-day Unleavened Bread celebration. The fact that Jesus is in Jerusalem and observing Passover is one more sign that Jesus is a faithful Jew. Jesus is obeying the requirement that all Jewish men celebrate this pilgrim feast in Jerusalem. Jesus instructs his disciples, "Go into the city to a certain man, and say to him, 'The Teacher says, "My time is near; I will keep the Passover at your house with my disciples.'" So, the disciples did as Jesus had directed them, and they prepared the Passover meal" (Matt 26:18–19).

In order to understand Jesus's words and actions at the Passover meal, it will be helpful to know a little about how that meal was celebrated. As we will see, Jesus *fulfills* the ritual of the Passover meal. That is, Jesus gives new meaning, an additional meaning, to what is taking place, just as Jesus has *fulfilled* the words of the prophets, giving them an additional level of meaning.

In Jesus's time, the meal had four parts, each accompanied by the drinking of wine mixed with water. In the first part, the host said a blessing over the cup and a blessing for the coming meal. In the second part, the people ate unleavened bread and green herbs. The Passover lamb was brought in, the meaning of the Passover meal was explained, and the first part of the Hallel was sung. *Hallel* means *to sing praise*. The first part of the Hallel was Psalm 113 and Psalm 114:1–8. These psalms sing God's praises and recall the exodus. In the third part of the meal the lamb was eaten with bitter herbs (a reminder of the bitterness of slavery in Egypt), a blessing was offered over the third cup of wine, and thanksgiving was offered for the Passover meal. With the fourth cup of wine, the second part of Hallel, Psalms 115 to 118, were sung. The verses in Psalm 118 include several of the Old Testament allusions that we have discussed previously. For instance, as the psalm ends, it proclaims:

> I thank you that you have answered me
> and have become my salvation.
> The stone that the builders rejected
> has become the chief cornerstone.
> This is the LORD's doing;
> it is marvelous in our eyes.
> This is the day that the LORD has made;
> let us rejoice and be glad in it.
> Save us, we beseech you, O LORD!
> O LORD, we beseech you, give us success!
> Blessed is the one who comes in the name of the LORD.
> We bless you from the house of the LORD.

The LORD is God,
  and he has given us light.
Bind the festal procession with branches,
  up to the horns of the altar.
You are my God, and I will give thanks to you;
  you are my God, I will extol you.
O give thanks to the LORD, for he is good,
  for his steadfast love endures forever. (Ps 118:21–29)

Matthew tells us that before Jesus suffered his agony in the garden, he and the disciples had sung Hallel: "When they had sung the hymn, they went out to the Mount of Olives" (Matt 26:30). Matthew's Jewish audience knew to what hymn Matthew was referring.

As Jesus gathers with his disciples for the Passover meal, his coming death is foremost in his mind. He has already spoken of his burial and that his "time is near." During the meal, he confronts Judas with his betrayal, and again refers to himself as the Son of Man: "The Son of Man goes as it is written of him, but woe to that one by whom the Son of Man is betrayed!" (Matt 26:24).

Matthew then tells us, "Jesus took a loaf of bread, and after blessing it he broke it, gave it to the disciples, and said, 'Take, eat; this is my body.' Then he took a cup, and after giving thanks he gave it to them, saying, 'Drink from it, all of you; for this is my blood of the covenant, which is poured out for many for the forgiveness of sins'" (Matt 26:26–28). Jesus is speaking in the context of God's covenant promises to the Israelites. He is speaking in the context of a lamb's blood having saved the firstborn of the Israelites from the final plague and his people having been saved from slavery to the Egyptians. Now, Jesus is saying that he is the lamb that will be sacrificed. It is his blood that is going to be shed, and the sacrifice of his body and blood will free people from slavery, not to other nations, but to sin. God's promises of a messiah and a kingdom are being fulfilled, but the kingdom is not limited just to the Israelites, it is "for many," and it is not a geopolitical kingdom. This kingdom is in heaven and on earth.

Christians understand this account to be describing the institution of the Eucharist, the sacrament through which Jesus remains with his people, feeds them on the journey, and enables them to stay united with him, to be part of the body of Christ. The earliest Christians, who were all Jews, did not give up their Passover celebration. Nor did they give up keeping the weekly Sabbath. However, in addition to those celebrations, they did gather in each other's homes on Sundays to celebrate the resurrection and to join themselves to the risen Christ by celebrating Eucharist. The Law and the prophets have not been abolished. They have been fulfilled.

Jesus's final words at the Passover meal are: "I tell you, I will never again drink of this fruit of the vine until that day when I drink it new with you in my Father's kingdom" (Matt 26:29). Jesus is once again affirming his teaching that there is life after death. He is going to be killed, but he will still be alive and with the disciples after his death and resurrection. They then sing the hymn (see Matt 26:30), the psalm that declares, "the stone that the builders rejected has become the chief cornerstone" (Ps 118:22); the hymn that proclaims, "Blessed is the one who comes in the name of the LORD" (Ps 118:26); the hymn that affirms, "This is the LORD's doing; it is marvelous in our eyes" (Ps 118:23). Jesus and his disciples then leave for the Mount of Olives.

JESUS'S PASSION, DEATH, AND BURIAL

As Jesus and the disciples arrive at the Mount of Olives, Jesus says, "You will all become deserters because of me this night; for it is written, 'I will strike the shepherd, / and the sheep of the flock will be scattered'" (Matt 26:31). Here Jesus is once more quoting the Book of Zechariah. The author speaks of a shepherd of the Lord being struck by a sword, causing the sheep, his followers, to scatter:

> "Awake, O sword, against the shepherd,
> against the man who is my associate,"
> says the LORD of hosts.
> Strike the shepherd, that the sheep may be scattered. (Zech 13:7)

This is what is going to happen to Jesus, the shepherd: People will come out to arrest him, armed with swords, and his disciples will all flee. Peter pledges never to desert Jesus. In response, Jesus tells Peter that he will deny him three times that very night.

Jesus withdraws with three of his disciples to Gethsemane, a small olive garden on the Mount of Olives, to pray. He is in great distress. He tells the disciples, "I am deeply grieved and agitated, even to death; remain here, and stay awake with me" (Matt 26:18). Then Jesus prays, "My Father, if it is possible, let this cup pass from me; yet not what I want but what you want" (Matt 26:39). Later he prays, "My Father, if this cannot pass unless I drink it, your will be done" (Matt 26:42). He prays again, a third time, using the "same words" (Matt 26:44). Notice that as Jesus prays, he is completely honest about his distress, as he was with his disciples. Still, he trusts his Father, and he still wants to do his Father's will. That is what is most important. This deep distress, honesty, and faith expressed in prayer are reminiscent of Psalms 42 and 43 (thought to have been originally one psalm and later divided), a personal lament in which the psalmist expresses both his suffering and his total trust in God. Three times the psalmist prays:

> Why are you cast down, O my soul,
>   and why are you disquieted within me?
> Hope in God; for I shall again praise him,
>   my help and my God. (Pss 42:5, 11; 43:5)

This psalmist experienced taunts, just as Jesus will. The psalmist says:

> Why must I walk about mournfully
>   because the enemy oppresses me?
> As with a deadly wound in my body,
>   my adversaries taunt me,
> while they say to me continually,
>   "Where is your God?" (Ps 42:9b–10)

Jesus, too, will be taunted in the same way. Matthew tells us that those who passed by the crucified Jesus said, "He trusts in God; let God deliver him now, if he wants to; for he said, 'I am God's Son'" (Matt 27:43).

After his agonizing yet faith-filled prayer, Jesus continues to accept what he knows to be his Father's will. He gets up, awakens the three disciples who failed to stay awake and support him, and faces his future with courage and purpose. Jesus says, "See, the hour is at hand, and the Son of Man is betrayed into the hands of sinners. Get up, let us be going" (Matt 26:46). It is then that Judas comes up to Jesus and kisses him.

When Judas and a large crowd armed with swords, including chief priests and elders, come to arrest him, Jesus is a model of his own teachings. Jesus does not want to be defended with swords. He admonishes one of his followers for attacking a slave of the high priest, cutting off his ear. Jesus knows that he is doing God's will and that he must endure the crucifixion. He says, "Do you think that I cannot appeal to my Father, and he will at once send me more than twelve legions of angels? But how then would the scripture be fulfilled, which says it must happen in this way?" (Matt 26:53–54). Jesus believes that the Jewish Scriptures are God's inspired word and that they guide people in God's way. He constantly expresses himself by quoting those Scriptures. He then says to the people, "But all this has taken place, so that the scriptures of the prophets may be fulfilled" (Matt 26:56). It is at this point that all the disciples desert Jesus. Zechariah's prophecy is being fulfilled: The shepherd has been struck, and the sheep have been scattered.

Jesus is then taken to the house of Caiaphas, the high priest. Jesus faces two charges: He threatened to destroy the Temple, and he claimed to be the Messiah, the Son of God. The high priest asks him directly: "I put you under oath before the living God, tell us if you are the Messiah, the Son of God" (Matt 26:63). In answer, Jesus once again alludes both to the Book of Daniel and to Psalm 110. Jesus says, "You have said so. But I tell you, from now on you will see the Son of Man seated at the right hand of Power and coming on the clouds of heaven" (Matt 26:64). We have often noted the passage from Daniel 7:13–14 in which Daniel sees one like a Son of Man coming on the clouds of heaven and receiving dominion, glory, and kingship from God. Every time Jesus refers to himself as the Son of Man he is alluding to this passage. That the Son of Man will sit "at the right hand of Power" is an allusion to Psalm 110, which begins: "The LORD says to my Lord / 'Sit at my right hand / until I make your enemies your footstool.'" As noted in chapter 6, Jesus quoted this passage earlier when he was challenging the Pharisees (see Matt 22:44), trying to expand their understanding of the Messiah.

The high priest is outraged and accuses Jesus of blasphemy. The scribes and elders who are present agree and give their verdict: "He deserves death" (Matt 26:66b). Their verdict is in accord with instructions given in the Book of Leviticus: "One who blasphemes the name of the LORD shall be put to death" (Lev 24:16). It is at this point that people start to taunt Jesus, saying, "Prophesy to us, you Messiah. Who is it that struck you?" (Matt 26:68). It is also at this point that Jesus's words to Peter that he would deny Jesus three times are fulfilled.

The chief priests and elders next take Jesus to Pilate who, as Roman procurator, had civil authority in Judea. Matthew interrupts his story of Jesus before Pilate by concluding the story of Judas's betrayal (see Matt 26:14–16). Judas, overcome by guilt, throws his thirty shekels of silver into the Temple and hangs himself. The chief priests use the money to buy the potter's field. The potter's field was originally the place where potters found the clay to make their pots. It became a burial ground not only for foreigners but for other marginalized people such as paupers and plague victims. As he concludes Judas's tragic story, Matthew includes his last fulfillment citation. He says, "Then was fulfilled what had been spoken through the prophet Jeremiah, 'And they took the thirty pieces of silver, the price of the one on whom a price had been set, on whom some of the people of Israel had set a price, and they gave them for the potter's field, as the Lord commanded me'" (Matt 27:9–10).

Scripture scholars debate why Matthew attributes these words to Jeremiah since the words are a conflation of images from Zechariah and Jeremiah. We have already mentioned the thirty pieces of silver thrown into the Temple as described in Zechariah 11:12–13. This "blood money," as the chief priests and elders refer to it, is combined with two images from Jeremiah: a potter and the purchase of a field in which a pot is buried.

The setting for the passages from Jeremiah is the time when Judah was under siege shortly before the Babylonian exile (587–537 BCE). God instructs Jeremiah to go to a potter's house. Jeremiah obeys the Lord and finds the potter re-forming a clay pot. Then God explains the meaning of what Jeremiah has seen. God says, "Can I not do with you, O house of Israel, just as this potter has done? says the LORD. Just like the clay in the potter's hand, so are you in my hand, O house of Israel" (Jer 18:6). God accuses the people of Judah of forsaking him by making offerings to false gods and by filling the land with the blood of the innocent. Jeremiah is to proclaim to the people that because of their infidelity, Judah will fall by the sword (see Jer 19). Soon after this prophecy, Judah was conquered by the Babylonians.

Later, God instructs Jeremiah to purchase a field. Since Judah is under siege, it doesn't seem a wise time to buy property. Still, Jeremiah does as God instructs him and purchases the field. God then instructs Jeremiah to put the deed of purchase in an earthenware pot and bury it in the field in order to preserve it. Once more, Jeremiah obeys God. Jeremiah's purchasing the field is a sign of faith that God will save God's people in the future, and Judah will someday be free again (see Jer 32:6–15). Jeremiah says, "Thus says the LORD of hosts, the God of Israel: Houses and fields and vineyards shall again be bought in this land" (Jer 32:15).

How ironic it is that the chief priests and elders do not want to put Judas's money in the Temple treasury because it is "blood money," so they purchase the potter's field, while they, at the same time, are themselves in the process of spilling innocent blood, Jesus's blood. Matthew emphasizes this fact by saying that the potter's field "has been called the Field of Blood to this day" (Matt 27:8).

Matthew next returns to his account of Jesus being questioned by Pilate. Pilate first asks Jesus, "Are you the King of the Jews?" (Matt 27:11). Notice, this is a different question from "Are you the Messiah?" Jesus claiming to be a messiah would not necessarily be seditious because the Messiah, the Anointed One, could be a priest or prophet, not necessarily a king. Claiming to be a king would be a direct threat to rulers appointed by Rome. Jesus gives an ambiguous answer: "You say so" (Matt 27:11). These are Jesus's last words to Pilate. When asked other questions, Jesus remains silent. Jesus's silence is evocative of the Suffering Servant in Isaiah's Suffering Servant songs. We have previously noted that these songs were later applied to Jesus. When describing the Suffering Servant, that is, the nation Israel personified, Isaiah says:

> He was oppressed, and he was afflicted,
> yet he did not open his mouth;
> like a lamb that is led to the slaughter,
> and like a sheep that before its shearers is silent,
> so he did not open his mouth. (Isa 53:7)

Jesus's choice of silence would also remind Matthew's Jewish audience of Psalm 38:

> Those who seek my life lay their snares;
> those who seek to hurt me speak of ruin,
> and meditate treachery all day long.
>
> But I am like the deaf, I do not hear;
> like the mute, who cannot speak.
> Truly I am like one who does not hear,
> and in whose mouth is no retort. (Ps 38:12–14)

After asking the crowd whom they wanted him to release during the festival time, Jesus or Barabbas, and declaring that he sees no guilt in Jesus, Pilate succumbs to the crowd's demands because he fears a riot. Pilate tries to exonerate himself by washing his hands before the crowd and saying, "I am innocent of this man's blood; see to it yourselves" (Matt 27:24). Pilate's Jewish onlookers would have understood the symbolism of this act. In Deuteronomy we read what the Israelites were to do if they found a dead body lying in open country but had no idea who was responsible for killing the person. They were to kill a heifer as a scapegoat, that is, to take the place of the unknown murderer. Then they were to wash their hands over the heifer and say, "'Our hands did not shed this blood, nor were we witnesses to it. Absolve, O Lord, your people Israel, whom you redeemed; do not let the guilt of innocent blood remain in the midst of your people Israel.' Then they will be absolved of blood guilt" (Deut 21:7–8).

The psalmists also sing of washing their hands to express their innocence. In Psalm 26, the psalmist asks the Lord for vindication because he believes he is innocent. He says:

> I wash my hands in innocence,
>   and go around your altar, O LORD,
> singing aloud a song of thanksgiving,
>   and telling all your wondrous deeds. (Ps 26:6–7)

In Psalm 73 the psalmist claims his innocence while he is being oppressed by wicked people:

> All in vain I have kept my heart clean
>   and washed my hands in innocence.
> For all day long I have been plagued,
>   and am punished every morning. (Ps 73:13–14)

In response to Pilate's false claim of innocence, the crowd responds, "His blood be upon us and on our children!" (Matt 27:25). This expression, a blood curse, also has Old Testament roots. In 2 Samuel 1:1–16 we read the story of a young man coming to David and telling him that both King Saul and his son, Jonathan, are dead. David asks the young man, a resident alien, how Saul died. The young man tells David that Saul had been injured and wanted to die. He asked the young man to kill him. The young man did as requested. On hearing this, David does not reward the resident alien for doing as Saul requested and for bringing Saul's crown to David. Rather, David condemns him to death. David says, "Your blood be on your head; for your own mouth has testified against you saying, 'I have killed the LORD's anointed'" (2 Sam 1:16). Like Pilate, those in the crowd were going to have blood on their hands and heads because they were all complicit in killing the Lord's anointed.

Another blood curse appears in 1 Kings. Solomon, David's son, has now become king. Joab, a general in David's army, had, without David's knowledge, killed two innocent men. He tries to seek sanctuary but is not granted it because the deaths were not accidental but intentional. King Solomon orders that Joab be killed, saying, "So shall their blood [that is, the two innocent men's blood] come back on the head of Joab and on the head of his descendants forever" (1 Kgs 2:33). In both of these instances, people in authority pronounce blood curses on guilty men for killing people who are innocent. In Matthew's account, the guilty, those in the crowd, are cursing themselves.

Matthew's description of the soldiers mocking Jesus as King of the Jews, crucifying him, and dividing Jesus's clothes among themselves (see Matt 27:27–37) recalls Psalm 22:

> For dogs are all around me;
>   a company of evildoers encircles me.
> My hands and feet have shriveled;
> I can count all my bones.
> They stare and gloat over me;
> they divide my clothes among themselves,
>   and for my clothing they cast lots. (Ps 22:16–18)

In fact, as we mentioned in our prologue, Matthew pictures Jesus praying Psalm 22. If I were writing about someone in agony, and I described him as saying, "Our Father, who art in heaven," you would know that I was not picturing that person saying only that one line. I was picturing him praying the Our Father. Matthew, too, is picturing Jesus praying Psalm 22. The psalm expresses not only Jesus's suffering, but also his faith in God's presence and love. Finally, the psalm names the significance of the crucifixion, what God is accomplishing through Jesus's passion and death.

In other words, Psalm 22 functions as midrash. As we described in our chapter on the infancy narratives, midrash is a literary device through which the author adds plot elements to his account of events. The plot elements are allusions to Old Testament texts. These Old Testament texts cast light on the significance of the events that are being described.

Here, in its entirety, is the psalm Jesus is pictured praying as his last act just before he dies:

> My God, my God, why have you forsaken me?
> Why are you so far from helping me,
>   from the words of my groaning?

O my God, I cry by day, but you do not answer;
   and by night, but find no rest.

Yet you are holy,
   enthroned on the praises of Israel.
In you our ancestors trusted;
   they trusted and you delivered them.
To you they cried, and were saved;
   in you they trusted, and were not put to shame.

But I am a worm, and not human;
   scorned by others, and despised by the people.
All who see me mock at me;
   they make mouths at me, they shake their heads;
"Commit your cause to the LORD; let him deliver—
   let him rescue the one in whom he delights!"

Yet it was you who took me from the womb;
   you kept me safe on my mother's breast.
On you I was cast from my birth,
   and since my mother bore me you have been my God.
Do not be far from me,
   for trouble is near
   and there is no one to help.

Many bulls encircle me,
   strong bulls of Bashan surround me;
they open wide their mouths at me,
   like a ravening and roaring lion.

I am poured out like water,
   And all my bones are out of joint;
my heart is like wax;
   it is melted within my breast;
my mouth is dried up like a potsherd,
   and my tongue sticks to my jaws;
   you lay me in the dust of death.

For dogs are all around me;
  a company of evildoers encircles me.
My hands and feet have shriveled;
I can count all my bones.
They stare and gloat over me;
they divide my clothes among themselves,
  and for my clothing they cast lots.

But you, O Lord, do not be far away!
  O my help, come quickly to my aid!
Deliver my soul from the sword,
  my life from the power of the dog!
  Save me from the mouth of the lion!

From the horns of the wild oxen you have rescued me.
I will tell of your name to my brothers and sisters;
  In the midst of the congregation I will praise you:
You who fear the Lord, praise him!
  All you offspring of Jacob, glorify him;
  stand in awe of him, all you offspring of Israel!
For he did not despise or abhor
  the affliction of the afflicted;
he did not hide his face from me,
  but heard when I cried to him.

From you comes my praise in the great congregation;
  my vows I will pay before those who fear him.
The poor shall eat and be satisfied;
  those who seek him shall praise the Lord.
  May your hearts live forever!

All the ends of the earth shall remember
  and turn to the Lord;
and all the families of the nations
  shall worship before him.
For dominion belongs to the Lord,
  and he rules over the nations.

To him, indeed, shall all who sleep in the earth bow down;
before him shall bow all who go down to the dust,
and I shall live for him.
Posterity will serve him;
future generations will be told about the LORD,
and proclaim his deliverance to a people yet unborn,
saying that he has done it.

This psalm on Jesus's lips expresses his terrible suffering. It recalls God's holiness and God's saving acts through history, saving acts that are coming to their culmination as Jesus prays. These saving acts will result not only in all of Jacob's offspring glorifying God, but in all the nations of the earth worshipping God. Indeed, all future generations will be told about the Lord's saving acts, the salvation of the whole human race, which was accomplished through Jesus, the Son of David, the Son of Man, the Anointed One, the Christ.

When Jesus cries out in prayer, some bystanders think that he might be calling for Elijah (Matt 27:47). As we already know, Elijah was expected to return to earth and prepare the way for the expected Messiah. From noon until 3:00 p.m., darkness covered the land. This recalls passages from both Exodus and Amos. In Exodus, during the ninth plague, darkness covered the earth for three days (Exod 10:22). Amos, an eighth-century-BCE prophet of God's justice, describes a day when God will come and judge those who are abusing the poor:

On that day, says the Lord GOD,
I will make the sun go down at noon,
and darken the earth in broad daylight. (Amos 8:9)

At Jesus's death, "The earth shook, and the rocks were split. The tombs also were opened, and many bodies of the saints who had fallen asleep were raised" (Matt 27:51b–52). This description evokes memories of passages in the Books of both Ezekiel and Isaiah. In Ezekiel, God instructs Ezekiel to say to the people, "Thus says the Lord GOD: I am going to open your graves and bring you up from your graves, O my people; and I will bring you back to the land of Israel. And you shall know that I am the LORD, when I open your graves, and bring you up from your graves, O my people. I will put my spirit within you, and you shall live" (Ezek 37:12–14). Isaiah, too, when prophesying that Israel would rise again, says,

> Your dead shall live, their corpses shall rise.
> O dwellers in the dust, awake and sing for joy!
> For your dew is a radiant dew,
> and the earth will give birth to those long dead. (Isa 26:19)

In both Ezekiel and Isaiah, the phrases "Open your graves" and "these corpses shall rise" are offering hope for the rebirth of the nation. In Matthew, tombs opening and the dead rising teach that there is life after death for individual people. A belief in life after death, in resurrection, is being proclaimed. As we have already discussed, some of the Jewish people had begun to believe in life after death about two hundred years before Jesus, well after Isaiah (742–701 BCE) and Ezekiel. (Remember, Ezekiel offered hope to the Israelites before and at the beginning [593–571 BCE] of the Babylonian exile.) The possibility of life after death was still a controversial topic in Jesus's time.

How ironic it is that the first act of faith after these truly earthshaking events comes from a Roman soldier. He says, "Truly this man was God's Son" (Matt 27:54). Jesus, the fulfillment of God's promises to the Israelites, has come to save all nations from slavery to sin and, in time, is going to be recognized by all nations.

After Jesus is taken down from the cross, he is buried. Mary Magdalene and Mary, the mother of James and Joseph, watch as Jesus is laid in the tomb by Joseph of Arimathea. A great stone is placed against the door of the tomb. Later, the chief priests and Pharisees seal the stone on the tomb because they do not want Jesus's disciples to steal the body and claim that Jesus has risen from the dead. This is reminiscent of the account of Daniel being put in the lion's den. Daniel was being punished for praying to his own God rather than praying to the king, which was required by law. After Daniel was thrown into the lion's den, "A stone was brought and laid on the mouth of the den, and the king sealed it with his own signet and with the signet of his lords, so that nothing might be changed concerning Daniel" (Dan 6:17). God saved Daniel by shutting the lions' mouths. The king was so astonished and amazed that he started to believe in Daniel's God too. He sent out a decree that

> in all my royal dominion people should tremble and fear before the God of Daniel:
> For he is the living God
> enduring forever.
> His kingdom shall never be destroyed,
> and his dominion has no end. (Dan 6:26)

HE IS RISEN!

As Matthew begins to tell us of Jesus's resurrection, he no longer uses any fulfillment citations to demonstrate how Jesus's life and ministry fulfilled the words of the prophets. Rather, he demonstrates how Jesus's own words about himself are now being fulfilled. As we know, Jesus had told his disciples that he would be killed, but, after three days, he would rise from the dead. When Mary Magdalene and the other Mary come to the tomb after the Sabbath (they come on Sunday morning; Jesus was crucified on Friday), there is once more a great earthquake. An angel descends from heaven, rolls back the stone, and sits on it. The angel says to the women, "I know that you are looking for Jesus who was crucified. He is not here; for he has been raised, as he said" (Matt 28:5). "As he said." Jesus's words were not empty promises. They were not hopeful dreams. Jesus's words have been fulfilled. Jesus is risen!

The angel then instructs the women to be witnesses of this good news. The angel tells them, "Go quickly and tell his disciples, 'He has been raised from the dead, and indeed he is going ahead of you to Galilee; there you will see him'" (Matt 28:7). It is in Galilee that Jesus grew up (in the small town of Nazareth; see Matt 21:11), where he began his public ministry, where he gave his Sermon on the Mount, and where Peter, James, and John witnessed the transfiguration.

As the women hurry away, they encounter Jesus himself: "They came to him, took hold of his feet, and worshipped him" (Matt 28:9). Praise and honor can be given to many. Worship is reserved for God.

Jesus then repeats the instructions that the women had received from the angel.

Matthew does not tell us about the interaction between the women and the disciples. The first thing he tells us is that the disciples went to the mountain in Galilee. They, too, worshipped Jesus. Jesus's last words to the disciples (also Matthew's last words to his readers) are: "All authority in heaven and on earth has been given to me. Go therefore and make disciples of all nations, baptizing them in the name of the Father and of the Son and of the Holy Spirit, and teaching them to obey everything that I have commanded you. And remember, I am with you always, to the end of the age" (Matt 28:18–20).

The risen Christ says that all authority has been given to him. Remember that Jesus has constantly referred to himself as the Son of Man, an allusion to the Book of Daniel. In Daniel, God gives the Son of Man

> dominion
> and glory and kingship,
> that all peoples, nations, and languages
> should serve him.
> His dominion is an everlasting dominion
> that shall not pass away,
> and his kingship is one
> that shall never be destroyed. (Dan 7:14)

Jesus claimed authority not only by calling himself the Son of Man but also in his teaching in his Sermon on the Mount. Remember, Jesus said, "You have heard that it was said.... But I say..." over and over. The question of Jesus's authority to "fulfill" the Law and the prophets loomed large in the mind of Matthew's contemporary Jews. Once more, Matthew is teaching that Jesus's words to his disciples have been fulfilled.

Jesus then commissions his disciples to make disciples of all nations. Remember, earlier when instructing the disciples, he had told them to go to their fellow Jews first (Matt 10:5–6; see also 15:24). Now the instructions are to go to all nations. The kingdom over which Jesus has authority is not a geopolitical kingdom. It is not even limited to all nations on earth. Jesus has initiated an eternal kingdom that already exists in heaven and will be established on earth as Jesus's disciples enjoin all nations to obey Jesus's teachings. One of those teachings is to pray that God's kingdom come, that God's will be done, on earth as it is in heaven (Matt 6:9–10). Jesus words have been, and are being, fulfilled.

The disciples are to baptize all nations in the name of the Father, Son, and Holy Spirit. These instructions recall Jesus's baptism. When Jesus was baptized by John, the Spirit descended upon him and the Father's voice said, "This is my Son, the Beloved, with whom I am well pleased" (Matt 3:17). The risen Christ, the Son of God, is one with the Father and the Holy Spirit.

Jesus's final words, "Remember, I am with you always, to the end of the age" (Matt 28:20) take us back to the annunciation to Joseph. Recall what the angel said to Joseph:

> "Joseph, son of David, do not be afraid to take Mary as your wife, for the child conceived in her is from the Holy Spirit. She will bear a son, and you are to name him Jesus, for he will save his people from their sins." All this took place to fulfill what had been spoken by the Lord through the prophet: "Look, the virgin shall conceive and bear a son, / and they shall name him Emmanuel," which means, "God is with us." (Matt 1:20–23)

The resurrected Christ is assuring his disciples that he is, indeed, Emmanuel; he is, indeed, God's son, and he will be with them always as they proclaim the kingdom of God to all nations.

Matthew is teaching his primarily Jewish contemporaries that Jesus is the fulfillment of God's promises to them. God's promises to Abraham, to David, and to their descendants have been fulfilled in Jesus. The prophets' words through the centuries have been fulfilled in Jesus. Jesus's words to his disciples and to the crowds during his public ministry have been fulfilled.

The living gospel through the centuries has been, and is, teaching all nations and all generations, including our generation, these same truths: Jesus has risen! Jesus remains with us! Jesus is God's own Son. We are to listen to him. We, too, are being invited to recognize who Jesus is and to follow his teachings. We are to love God with our whole heart, soul, and might (Deut 6:5), and we are to love our neighbor as ourselves (Lev 19:18). This is the heart of the good news, the Gospel according to Matthew.

SCRIPTURE INDEX